NatureCrafts

NatureCrafts

Seasonal Projects from Natural Materials

Mary Elizabeth Johnson

and

Katherine Pearson

OXMOOR HOUSE, INC. Birmingham

Eugene Butler	*Chairman of the Board*
Emory Cunningham	*President and Publisher*
Vernon Owens, Jr.	*Senior Executive Vice President*

*Conceived, edited, and published by Oxmoor House, Inc.,
under the direction of:*

Don Logan	*Vice President and General Manager*
Gary E. McCalla	*Editorial Director*
John Logue	*Editor-in-Chief*
Mary Elizabeth Johnson	*Senior Editor, Crafts*
Candace N. Conard	*Editor, Crafts*
Mary Jo Sherrill	*Associate Editor, Crafts*
Jerry Higdon	*Production Manager*

NATURECRAFTS

Editor: Candace N. Conard
Design: Viola Andrycich
Cover photograph and design: Steve Logan
Photography: Robert Perron, Steve Logan, David Matthews, John O'Hagen,
   Mike Clemmer, Sylvia Martin, Bob Lancaster, Tom Hagood, and Emilie Mims
Illustrations: Esther Lee, Don Smith

Special thanks to the staff of *Decorating & Craft Ideas*₍ₓ₎, especially to Charlotte Hagood, Merri C. Gow, Conchita R. Berry, Sara Jane Ball, Patti Hammond, Jane Mentzer, and Cynthia Rogers for their technical assistance.

Library of Congress Catalog Number: 79-83705
ISBN: 0-8487-0494-0
Manufactured in the United States of America
First Printing 1980

CONTENTS

INTRODUCTION

Mother Nature produces a unique harvest of craft materials at each season of the year. As we become more aware of the abundance of materials available to us, we begin to feel like a vegetable gardener overwhelmed by his bounty. It is as though the earth opens up and spills out an unceasing variety of textures, shapes, and colors that are not only beautiful in themselves, but also perfect for crafts projects of all types.

One of the joys of *NatureCrafts* is seeking and finding the materials. Train your eye to spot the possibilities around you and you will be amazed at what you find. Leafless twigs and branches in winter become dramatic arrangements. Drifts of seashells on summer beaches beg to be nestled in a bowl or basket on your coffee table. The vines you clean off your back fence in early spring make striking baskets, vases, or wreaths for your front door. Driving along a roadway cut through a hill or mountain, you may recognize different layers of natural clay and long to capture the clear colors in pots for your home. An early snow may draw you and your family outside to make snow people, including angels!

Subtly, we become aware that we can preserve special moments of our lives with keepsakes from nature. Twist a wreath of vines to recall a walk through the woods. Weave a basket from materials within arm's length on an afternoon picnic in the park. Preserve the delicate beauty of wildflower bouquets to enjoy all year. The fragrance of a summer evening is captured in potpourris and rose oils. A nodding seed head, ripe to bursting, or a capricious milkweed pod gently held in a lacy weaving lasts indefinitely, reminding us of when and where we found it.

Some of our dearest memories are made of those things which cannot be preserved at all. Temporal naturecrafts afford a great deal of pleasure in the tradition of mud pies, bamboo whistles, and straw forts. When children play, they adapt whatever materials are available to the game at hand. Open your eyes and play as children do. Ice panels and icicle cities, clover chains and passion flower dolls—all are rewarding afternoon diversions with Mother Nature.

All of the people who worked on this book have succumbed to the discreet charm of *NatureCrafts*. We've found ourselves elbow-deep in paper making even though there was a deadline pressing. The typesetter demands to know when the book will be ready so he can create the crafts he has been reading about. Friends, family, and passersby have caught our enthusiasm and have begun stuffing lamp bases with seashells, decorating their homes with cornhusk flowers, and refusing to give a gift unless it's a naturecraft. It's contagious!

We have selected some projects that offer surprises; some may hold answers to questions you have asked yourself about collecting and preserving. We've provided identification charts where possible to help you become more knowledgeable about the materials with which you are working. Our goal has been to alter the natural material as little as possible in the final product; we want to celebrate the beauty of the material itself. For this reason, we have done very little with paint or with finished wood.

It is our hope that you will not only learn new skills by doing the projects in this book, but that you will also begin to observe the world with a fresh awareness. There is an excitement in working with natural materials, and we wish for you to feel the delight we have all felt in becoming more aware of our environment and Nature's master plan. There is, without question, a spiritual reward to be enjoyed as well as the physical one of making something with your hands.

One word of earnest caution must be added: The balance of nature is delicate and must be protected. It is unfortunate, but all the danger to our environment cannot be blamed on industry. Sea oats, for example, were seriously diminished before protection by law because too many admirers wanted to enjoy the graceful stalks in their homes. Gardeners often unwittingly endanger wildflowers by attempting to transplant them. We encourage—no, beg—you to establish a rapport with your nearest nature center or conservation group; they can advise you of species in your area that are legally protected or dangerously scarce.

In support of responsible collecting, we have concentrated on projects that can be created from the most common materials, either found or cultivated. But even with the most plentiful materials, take only what you can use right away and never take all from one spot; leave at least one-half of the plants in each stand to go to seed and replenish themselves.

Nature and crafts—there is personal satisfaction and peace of mind to be gained from each. In seeking out a natural material, in holding it, and in working with it, you cannot help appreciating its distinct properties and subtleties. We hope this book will be the start of a fascinating adventure for you that will lead to a comfortableness with, a respect for, and a reassurance of Nature's inestimable order.

SpringCrafts

Natural Dyes for Easter Eggs

The Pennsylvania Dutch, who originated the Easter Bunny tradition in the eighteenth century, dyed eggs with wild berries, bark, grasses, and roots. Their idea of colored eggs hidden by the Easter Bunny is now firmly established as an American tradition, but their clever natural dyes unfortunately have been replaced with commercial tablets.

There is a noticeable difference in clarity and softness of color between eggs dyed with natural materials and eggs dyed with commercial tablets. For instance, the cabbage-dyed blue looks like a real bluebird's egg.

In addition to the roots, bark, wildflowers and berries you find outdoors in the spring, your spice shelf, vegetable bin, and freezer are also interesting sources for nature's colors. The colors that will result from natural dyeing are not always predictable, but it is that element of surprise which adds to the fun.

GENERAL PROCEDURE

In general, fresh fruits, leaves, roots, or berries give better color than an equal amount of commercially frozen or canned material. Chop, shred, or crush 1 or more cups of fresh dyestuff or measure out 2 tablespoons or more of dried spices.

Place dyestuff in a glass, ceramic, or enamel pot with 4 cups of water; simmer for 30 minutes or more to extract color. Strain liquid to remove dyestuff.

Dip clean, white eggs into the dye, making certain that the eggs are completely covered by the liquid. For pale tints, use pre-cooked eggs. For deep shades, cook eggs directly in dyestuff. Simmer eggs for 20 minutes or until desired color has been achieved. Turn eggs often during dyeing process to prevent spotting when the egg rests against the sides or bottom of the container.

When dyed, remove eggs from the dye bath and place on paper towels or a rack to dry, turning them at least once to prevent spotting. Some colors may continue to develop and change after drying.

Note: The shells of commercially processed eggs may have been coated with an oily film to retard spoilage. This coating may also resist the dye and should be removed by wiping the egg with a solution of 1 tablespoon white vinegar to 1 cup of water. Rinse to remove this solution; then dry the egg. The same vinegar water solution can be used to scrub the color from "mistakes," allowing eggs to be re-dyed in a second solution.

NATURAL COLORS

With the procedure above, several vegetable substances were found to be particularly intriguing as dyestuffs. In some cases, dye quality was improved by adding 1 teaspoon of either alum (available at grocery stores) or white vinegar to the dyestuff.

Pecan or Hickory Bark for toasty beige color.
Madder Root for light red.
Paprika for pale rusty brown.
Alder Catkins for yellow.
Instant Coffee and Walnut Hulls for deep, rich brown.
Dried Sassafras Root: 1 teaspoon vinegar per 1 cup dye for medium to deep rusty orange.
Fresh Red Cabbage: 1 teaspoon alum per 1 cup dye for deep sapphire blue to medium blue.
Dried Turmeric: 1 teaspoon vinegar per 1 cup dye for bright yellow.
Frozen Blueberries for pale gray blue.
Onion Skins for yellow orange.
Red Onion Skins for pale blue.

Note: Successive dyeings in the same cup of liquid will produce a variety of shades until the color is exhausted. Try other fresh, edible roots, berries, barks, or flowers, using alum or vinegar to vary the color and help set the dye.

Handle eggs carefully after dyeing since some colors are only weakly absorbed by the eggshell and are easily scratched and chipped.

WRAPPING

An alternative method of coloring eggs, which was used for those eggs nestled in the flowers shown on page 3, is to wrap the dyeing material, such as onion skin, red cabbage, or grasses, around the egg and then tie the egg securely in cheesecloth.

Boil the eggs for 10 to 15 minutes in clear water; then remove the cheesecloth. A mottled effect will be achieved. You can control the mottling by choosing carefully the placement of the skins or by placing something such as a fern frond or a plant's seed head between the egg and the onion skin.

EASTER BASKET FOR NATURAL-DYED EGGS

The moss-covered basket shown in the photograph is the perfect complement to the soft colors of the Easter Eggs. The basket is made by simply glueing sheet sphagnum moss onto the outside of a plastic bowl. Drill two holes on opposite sides of the bowl so that a twig handle can be attached with florist's wire. Make the handle from several small branches that have no leaves, tying the branches together in several places with florist's wire. The inside of the bowl is unfinished, but sheet sphagnum moss could be glued there as well.

Pots from Local Clay

In the eighteenth and nineteenth centuries, clay attracted a kind of boom-town community as itinerant potters settled near natural deposits. The Jugtown Potters of North Carolina and a few potters in Georgia and Alabama are the last of the family industries centered around local clay. A few university-trained potters are beginning to experiment with local clays, so sources of natural clay are drawing potters to the South, where large deposits are common.

Before the Europeans introduced them to the wheel, American Indians made pottery by building up thin coils of clay and then smoothing the sides to eliminate the coil pattern. Making a pot in this way allows you to work with the clay right from the ground, thus retaining its natural color, which would be muddied by mixing or wedging.

Clay can be found throughout the United States in limited supplies but in surprising colors—peach to terra cotta, iron red, chalky white, and soft gray. You need only a little clay to make indigenous pottery without a wheel.

DIGGING THE CLAY

Since vegetation does not grow well in clay, it is usually easy to find deposits. Look for bare spots in a field, along the highway, or on a river bank. Clay is shiny and breaks up in chunks rather than fine particles when you dig into it. You can simplify your hunt by phoning the geological survey department in your area. They can tell you if clay is available nearby and where the most promising spots are.

The best time to dig clay is after a good, hard, soaking rain. If you dig the clay dry, wet it thoroughly

before working with it. Clean out any small stones that will cause the pot to explode in the kiln, but do not mix or knead the clay at all. Kneading will turn the natural color a muddy brown.

Materials
local clay
clear ceramic glaze

Equipment
rolling pin   knife
plate or bowl   paint scraper (4" wide)
kiln (Ceramic shops that sell greenware will often fire
   your pieces for a fee.)

SHAPING THE POT
Pack several chunks of wet clay into a ball; compress the clay as tightly as possible to eliminate air bubbles, which can cause the pot to crack in firing. With a rolling pin, roll the ball of clay out as you would a pie crust, but keep the clay slab ⅜" to ½" thick. Choose a bowl or round plate of the diameter you'd like the finished pot to be, and turn it upside down over the clay slab; the plate will serve as a pattern to make the base of the pot perfectly round. With a knife, cut through the clay all the way around the plate. Then remove the plate and excess clay from the round base.

Gather another handful of wet clay. With the open palm of your hand, roll the clay back and forth on a flat surface to form a thick coil. Wrap this coil around the outside edge of the base slab and continue building up more coils, one on top of another, until the sides are the height you want.

With a wide paint scraper, smooth the sides of the pot until the coils are no longer apparent. Cut the top coil into a flat, hard edge. At this stage, the pot will be a muddy, unattractive color because the outside surface of the clay has been mixed in making the coils and smoothing the sides.

FINISHING
Let the pot dry overnight or longer until the clay is firm and no longer tacky. Then use a knife to scrape away the thin, muddy surface layer, revealing the pure color of the clay underneath. Dry the pot for several more days before firing in a kiln at 2000° F. (Firing at a temperature above 2000° F. will darken the terra cotta pots to a brown tone.)

To keep the true color, the clay must not be kneaded or wedged. By eliminating these steps, however, the chances of breakage in the kiln are increased. Air bubbles, stones, and moisture in the clay will explode in firing. Make sure the pot is completely dry before firing it in the kiln.

After the first firing, apply a clear ceramic glaze to intensify the natural color; then fire the pot again.

Ash-Dried Fruit

Fruits such as oranges, tangerines, grapefruit, and honeydews can be transformed into containers remarkably like pottery through a slow, carefully monitored drying process. Because the technique uses wood ashes, late spring is the perfect time to try this craft—that seems to be when everyone cleans out the fireplace or wood stove. You may find that you need more ashes than you can provide just by yourself, so offer to clean out your neighbor's fireplace as well! This craft will lead you on and on out of fascination with what the next fruit will look like when dried! The drying process takes from 1 to 2 months, depending on the weather and the size of the fruit.

Materials
oranges
lemons
grapefruit
tangerines
any melon
pumpkins
dry, wood ashes
olive oil
beeswax

Equipment
covered container to
  store ashes
knife
spoon
string
toothbrush

CLEANING AND PREPARING

You must replenish the wood ashes often, so you'll need a large supply. Store the ashes in a galvanized garbage can with a lid. Choose perfectly formed fruit without blemishes or soft spots. With the knife on a slant, cut a top out of the fruit as you would cut a pumpkin when making a jack-o-lantern. Use a spoon to gently remove all the inside of the fruit; scrape the inside of melons until scrapings become inedible. Be very careful not to tear the edges of the opening or to puncture the rind.

Fill the melons and fruit with dry, wood ashes. (Always work outside; the fine powdery ash is difficult to remove indoors.) If you want a covered container, replace the top and wrap the fruit over and over with string as if you were winding a ball of yarn. Grapefruit and thick-skinned oranges make the most successful covered containers.

Of the pieces shown here, the large honeydew melon, the orange with a "collar," and the grapefruit half were turned inside out at one point in the drying process. Inverting allows you to achieve a rolled lip or contrasting textures. But only those pieces that have been perfectly cut and hollowed without any damage to the cut edge or the rind can be turned inside out. From the beginning, rub olive oil into the cut edges of those pieces you want to turn inside out. Repeat applications of oil every few days to prohibit fast drying of the edge, which will make it too brittle to turn later.

DRYING

Put the fruits in a dry place and change the wood ashes daily for the first week or so and after that as necessary. In humid weather, the fruits may require new ashes daily throughout the entire drying process. Mold or an odor of rotting indicates that the ash is not being changed often enough. Each time you dump and replenish the wood ashes, you must retie the covered containers as tightly as possible.

The fruits and melons will go through three noticeable stages as they dry—from crisp while still relatively fresh, through a leathery stage, to a hard surface when completely dry.

TURNING INSIDE-OUT

It is during the leathery stage that you must turn inside out those fruits you wish to give special character to. Each time you change the ash, gently work with the fruit to determine when it becomes tough but pliable. A tangerine may be leathery for only a day or so and should be turned right away, while pumpkins stay pliable for up to 2 weeks.

Turning the pieces inside out takes a great deal of patience, and even working slowly and cautiously, you may still tear a promising specimen. Once inside out, the lips of the fruits can be shaped to give them a vase form.

Refill the fruits with wood ashes and continue to change the ash until the inverted fruit is completely dry, reshaping the lip as often as necessary.

SEALING

When your fingernail clicks against a hard, dry surface after several weeks of drying, dump the wood ashes and brush out any remaining particles with a toothbrush.

Put the dried containers into a 200° F. oven, where they will soften and then harden again. If you need to improve the fit of covers or to reshape a lip or opening, pull a piece out of the oven (with gloves) while it is soft, rework it, and return it to the oven to harden.

Warm the beeswax and add to it just enough olive oil to make it workable. Rub this sweet-smelling wax over the inside and outside of the dried pieces to protect them from the humidity.

For a blackened "pot," such as the grapefruit shown in the photograph, return the fruit to a 400° F. oven after waxing. "Fire" it in the hot oven until it darkens.

If the finished "pots" should get wet on a windowsill or absorb too much moisture during rainy weather, put them back into a 200° F. oven to dry.

FELT:
Nature's Textile

Felting is a process that predates both spinning and weaving, making it one of the oldest known textile forms. It is believed that the origin of felt is closely connected both chronologically and geographically with the domestication of sheep, goats, and camels. Perhaps it was merely an astute observer with an active imagination who noticed the matted substance on the ground of the animals' enclosure. The wool had become damp, was warmed by the animal bodies, and then trampled flat by their hooves. This provided the three elements necessary for the felting process to occur: moisture, heat, and agitation. So animals themselves were the first felters!

The unknown discoverer of felt was probably a member of a nomadic tribe in Eurasia. Handmade felt in this part of the world was developed as a highly functional material and became a basic, essential element upon which life depended. It was used for shelter, clothing, footwear, rugs, blankets, bags, and even religious images. By far the most ingenious use of felt was as a covering for nomadic tents, or yurts. Yurts were round, collapsible structures traditionally covered with handmade felt and girded with handsomely patterned handwoven bands. The wool of approximately 190 sheep was used to make one yurt covering.

One of the first outside activities for the farmer in the earliest days of spring has always been sheep shearing. The thick, warm coat of the sheep is the wonderful wool we all treasure in its processed form of fabric or yarn. The ancient processes of cleaning, carding, spinning, and weaving all usually take place unseen by most of us—the distance from the farm and the time required to make our own fabric would probably prove discouraging to all but the most determined.

However, the process of felting provides us with a fairly quick and simple way to make woolen fabric. It bypasses the laborious steps necessary for weaving or knitting and requires no special skills or equipment. It is probably one of the purest of all naturecrafts.

BASIC STEPS

1. Choose fiber.
2. Prepare fiber.
3. Lay out encasement—a color-fast fabric other than wool that can be easily stitched through (old sheets are recommended).
4. Arrange fibers in layers on top of the encasement fabric. All the fibers in each layer should be roughly parallel to each other but not parallel to the layer superimposed on top of it. A minimum of three layers is recommended for sturdy felt. The layered fibers form a batt.
5. Wrap the encasement fabric around the fiber batt and secure according to the felting method you are using.
6. Felt using either the Stitched or the Chicago Tube Sock Method discussed on pages 10 and 11.
7. Dry in an automatic dryer or by air.

SELECTING THE WOOL

Several key points are basic to the felting process: 1) Wool loses approximately 40 percent of its strength when wet. Therefore, an encasing fabric is necessary and should be of a material other than wool, which might adhere to the new felt. It is important for a majority of the wool fibers to lie nearly at right angles within the encasement fabric and to have freedom of movement. 2) The felt-maker can expect about 33 to 50 percent shrinkage during the process. This percentage depends on the particular fiber and felting method chosen. Shrinkage will even vary from fleece to fleece, and it is best to make a test swatch, measure before and after the felting process, and duplicate exactly the test procedures during the actual felting process.

Wool used for felting may be found in one of several forms: raw wool, precarded batts, wool yarns, and even old clothes. A more complete discussion of these and other fibers for blended felt follows in chart form. (See Suppliers, page 150, if you do not have a source for raw wool.) The objects illustrated with this article are made from raw wool freshly sheared from sheep. This wool is called "in the grease."

Choosing quality raw wool calls for careful consideration. A good fleece should be fairly free of straw, feed, burrs, and other debris. It should not be matted or damp or have many "second cuts," which are short pieces, ½" or so, made when the shearer makes a second pass in an effort to leave less wool on the animal. The fleece should be nicely crimped, wavy, and from 2" to 4" in length.

Strength is also important and related to animal health. To check the fleece for strength, hold one lock of wool up to the light; if the animal has been sick, there will be a weak line across the fibers. One further test is to hold one end of the lock in each hand and pull; the lock should not break.

Once a good fleece has been chosen, do not store it in plastic (ask to be sure that it was not previously stored this way). Use paper or cloth bags, preferably suspended so that air can circulate freely around and through the fibers.

SCOURING RAW WOOL

It is necessary to clean, or "scour," raw wool before felting. This reduces the amount of shrinkage that will occur during felting. If maximum shrinkage were allowed to occur during the felting process, holes might form in the fabric. "Scouring" is a misleading term because it implies an active cleaning, whereas in the case of wool, scouring is a gentle process. Follow the directions explicitly for this procedure to avoid matting and premature felting.

Rinse No. 1: Fill a large sink or container with enough hot water to allow the wool to float freely. The water should be about 130° F. or so hot that your bare hands can hardly stay in it.

Drop the wool on top of the water and allow it to absorb water and sink to the bottom. (You may press lightly.) When the fibers are thoroughly saturated and the wool has sunk, begin timing the rinse for 10 minutes. Do not stir or agitate.

Hold the wool aside while draining water from the sink, or pour wool and water through a colander if you are using another type of container. Press the wool gently to aid in draining.

Rinse No. 2: Repeat Rinse No. 1. Do not run water directly onto the wool.

Wash No. 1: Remove the wool from the container and drain the water. Quickly—before the wool has time to cool—refill the container with 130° F. water. Keep an accurate account of the number of gallons of water added or mark the container ahead of time. Again, use enough water so that the wool will float freely.

Add 1 ounce (or 2½ tablespoons) Arm & Hammer Washing Soda® (in a blue and green box) for every 2 gallons of water. Be sure the washing soda is thoroughly dissolved before adding the wool. Drop the wool in; allow it to sink and remain for 5 minutes only. Drain as before.

Wash No. 2: Repeat Wash No. 1 and allow to soak for 5 minutes.

Rinse No. 3: Repeat Rinse No. 1.

Rinse No. 4: Repeat Rinse No. 1.

REMOVING EXCESS MOISTURE

Spread wool out on a towel and pat to remove as much water as possible.

Place damp wool in a pillowcase and run through the spin cycle of an automatic washing machine.

When moisture has been removed, spread wool out on a clean surface and allow it to air dry. If the wool is to be dyed, it should be done while it is wet, before it is spread out. Wool may be stored wet in the refrigerator if dyeing will take place within a few days.

FIBER SELECTION AND PREPARATION

Fiber	Preparation
Raw Wool Layered Carded Wool or Yarns Layered Fluffed Wool	Scour according to directions. Fluff wool by opening up clumps with your fingers and picking out any remaining debris. (This is called "teasing and picking.") Next, card with hand cards or drum carding machine if desired, or fluffed wool may be used as it is. Arrange in layers as directed in the Basic Steps. If carded wool is used, the layers of parallel fibers should be placed almost exactly perpendicular to each other.
Wool Top (Roving)	This is a long strand of commercially scoured and carded wool. Tear off appropriate lengths, open up, and spread into thin layers. Arrange in layers as directed in the Basic Steps.
Wool Batts	Also a commercially scoured and carded wool, usually in rectangular units. Arrange in layers as directed in the Basic Steps.
Wool Yarns	Cut desired lengths and layer as directed in the Basic Steps.
Wool Textile Products (old wool clothes)	For true, non-woven felt, these must be torn apart and shredded with fingers or carders. If you are not concerned with making "true" felt, the cloth may be cut into strips or shapes and combined with other wool.
Other Fibers: ginned cotton, cotton balls, raw silk, jute, sisal, flax, camel, goat, etc.—check your local zoo!	Preparation will depend on whether the fiber is raw or processed. There must always be at least 15 to 20 percent wool present in a blend for effective felting to occur.

STITCHED METHOD

This modern felting method uses both washing machine and dryer. It usually results in a very sturdy and heavily textured felt. Texture results from the stitching that holds the wool in place within the encasement fabric while the wool is being agitated.

Materials
prepared fiber
encasement fabric
thread
detergent

Equipment
straight pins
needle
seam ripper
washing machine and dryer

Encasement. Arrange the prepared fibers on the encasement fabric. Wrap them up (sandwich style) and pin.

Stitch. Hand stitch rows, close together, through the layers with stitches that are about ½" in length. It is best to stitch over the entire surface at first and then fill in the smaller spaces. (Diagram 1.) Open spaces should not be any wider than 1" when the stitching is completed. It is possible to stitch in subtle patterns, such as ribs or diagonals, which will show up in the finished felt.

Wash. After stitching is complete, place the batt in a washing machine with the normal amount of detergent (*not* a soap). Set the machine on hot wash and cold rinse. If such a setting is not available, wait until the machine has filled with hot water and change the temperature setting to cold. The regular or heavy-duty setting is best—the rougher the machine is on the wool, the stronger the felt will be.

Dry. After the complete wash and spin cycle, place the partially felted textile in a hot dryer on the regular cycle until it is dry—usually about 1 hour.

Test. With a seam ripper, rip out one corner of the casing and see if the felt is firm enough. If it is not, repeat the wash and dry cycles. If the felt is firm enough, continue ripping the casing off.

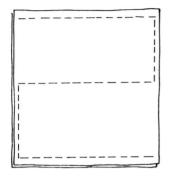

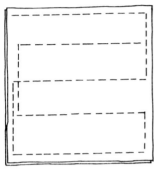

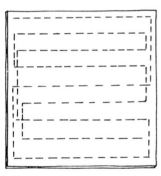

Diagram 1

Diagram 3

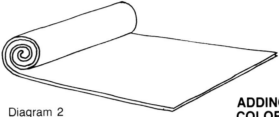

Diagram 2

CHICAGO TUBE SOCK METHOD

This method also uses a washing machine and dryer and usually results in felt with a striated texture. Developed as an alternative to the Stitched Method, it will yield a felt of similar sturdiness, although the texture and the shape of the felt are not as easily controlled.

Materials
prepared fiber
encasement fabric
thread
tube sock
string or rubber band
detergent

Equipment
needle
washing machine and dryer

Encasement. Wrap the layers of prepared fiber in the encasement fabric. If desired, stitch loosely for extra control and security.

Roll. Roll the encased fiber as though you were making a jelly roll. (Diagram 2.)

Stitch. If the batt was not stitched as it was placed in the encasement fabric, it may be stitched through in rolled form. Again, stitching at all in this method is optional.

Stuff. Stuff the rolled batt into a tube sock or a stocking leg, whichever is appropriate in size. (Diagram 3.) Make sure the roll of wool to be felted is pushed all the way to the toe of the sock. Tie the open end with string or a rubber band so that the batt will not slip out of the sock. It is also possible to stitch through the sock and batt at this point.

Wash. Place in the washing machine as directed in the Stitched Method.

Dry. Remove from sock, rip out any stitches, and unroll to place in dryer. Dry as directed in the Stitched Method.

Remove from casing.

ADDING TEXTURE AND COLOR

There are several ways to vary the design of your felt. The first four methods described here are ones that must be done to the fabric before you go through the felting process; dyeing, however, may be done either before or after the felting process.

Embed different materials between the layers of fibers—even things such as grass, ribbons, or straw.

Superimpose patterns on top of the layers or under the first layer. This can be done with yarns or any dyed wool textile products. The patterns you form can be geometric, figurative, abstract, impressionistic, or whatever.

Blend the wool fleece with other fibers—rayon, polyester, silk, cotton, flax, jute, animal hair, or cotton or metallic threads.

Layer different colors or forms of wool, or layer different fibers.

Dye the felt or fibers. Use household or natural dyes. There are also special dyes made for wool.

Try traditional fiber techniques with your felt fabric. Cut felt into pieces or strips and use the strips in basketry, weaving, crocheting, appliquéing, patchwork, quilting, or trapunto. Vests, coats, shirts, hats, bonnets, and jackets can be made from your own felt. Let the projects we show here get you started, but don't let them limit your imagination.

Felt Yogurt Warmer

This handy little kitchen item keeps your cultured milk, which you have heated to the boiling point, warm enough to allow it to become yogurt. In addition to being so useful, it is an excellent way to utilize scraps of felt leftover from other projects. The random seams in the warmer shown in the photograph are the result of piecing and were deliberately accented with crochet stitches.

Materials
felt or scraps of felt
quart jar with lid
assorted lengths of yarn in desired colors

Equipment
scissors
crewel needle
crochet hook

Cut felt following the shape and dimensions given in Diagram 3, or arrange felt scraps according to Diagram 3. Form the shape into a cylinder and fold the top down around the jar to make sure the warmer will fit.

With crewel needle and yarn, blanket-stitch along the edges of the piece of felt or along the edges of the scraps to be joined. (Diagram 1.) You may make the blanket stitches large and uneven, as shown in the photograph, for an unusual textural effect.

YOGURT RECIPE
1 quart milk
4 tablespoons unflavored yogurt with an active culture (Use your own after the first batch.)
¼ cup non-instant dry milk (Health food stores carry this.)

Scald milk in a 1½- or 2-quart saucepan and allow to cool to 115° F. (use a candy thermometer).

Beat in yogurt culture and dry milk with a whisk.

When all the solids have dissolved and mixture is well blended, pour liquid into the quart jar and wrap the jar in the yogurt warmer. (This recipe makes one quart of yogurt with some foamy milk left over.)

Place the wrapped jar in a warm spot and allow to stand for at least eight hours. During the last couple of hours, taste periodically and check for consistency. (The longer yogurt is allowed to develop, the more tart it will taste.) When the yogurt is ready, unwrap the jar and refrigerate.

Homemade yogurt will be less firm than the commercial variety. Flavor it with your choice of fresh fruit, preserves, honey, or nuts.

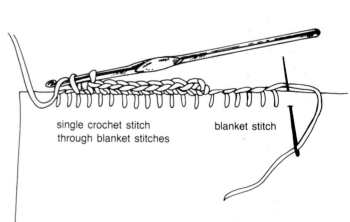

single crochet stitch
through blanket stitches

blanket stitch

Diagram 1

Bring the side edges to be joined together and crochet through the blanket stitches with a single crochet stitch. (Diagram 1.) Fold the top flap down and tuck it inside; then blanket-stitch it in place.

To make the bottom section, cut a circle of felt roughly the same size as the bottom of the jar. Cut another piece of felt according to the dimensions given in Diagram 2. The two points are where the ties will be attached. For added strength, stitch around both sides of the points with yarn as shown in the diagram.

Ease the unpointed edge of this strip onto the bottom circle of felt and stitch in place. The felt is quite pliable and will ease well. To make ties, thread the crewel needle with a double strand of yarn approximately 18″ long. Stitch ties securely to both of the points on the bottom of the yogurt warmer.

To use the warmer, tie the base section onto the jar full of yogurt, with the knot on the lid of the jar. Pull the top over the jar and allow the yogurt to stand for at least eight hours.

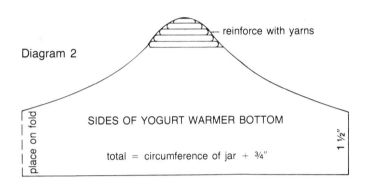

Diagram 2

reinforce with yarns

place on fold

SIDES OF YOGURT WARMER BOTTOM

total = circumference of jar + ¾″

1 ½″

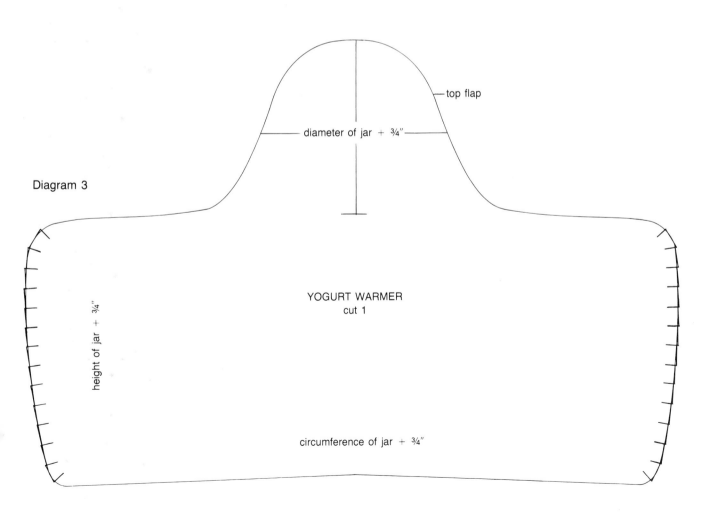

Diagram 3

top flap

diameter of jar + ¾″

YOGURT WARMER
cut 1

height of jar + ¾″

circumference of jar + ¾″

Felt Slippers

These slippers are perfect for keeping tootsies warm on nippy nights. Felt alone can be used for the soles if you expect to give the slippers light wear. But if heavy wear is expected, stitch on additional lightweight leather soles with a blanket stitch.

Materials
felt, fairly thick
knitting yarn

Equipment
paper pattern
scissors
crewel needle
crochet hook

Make a pattern for the soles of the slippers by tracing around your feet in a general outline that is at least 1″ larger all the way around each foot. Cut patterns for the toe and heel pieces according to the dimensions given in Diagrams 1 and 2. You may wish to reinforce the inside tip of the toe piece with darning stitches.

Attach the toe sections to the soles by tucking the raw edges to the inside and stitching by hand through the two layers.

Try the slippers on and position the heel sections. If the size needs decreasing, overlap the heel and toe sections at the seam by the required amount; increase the size by adding a crocheted seam between the heel and toe sections as described for the felt tea cozy.

Stitch the corner edges of the heel sections to the soles. Stitch the heel sections to the toe sections at the seam. Blanket stitch (Diagram 1, page 12) around the open edges of the slipper, as shown on the diagrams, and finish off with two or three rows of single crochet. (Diagram 1, page 12.)

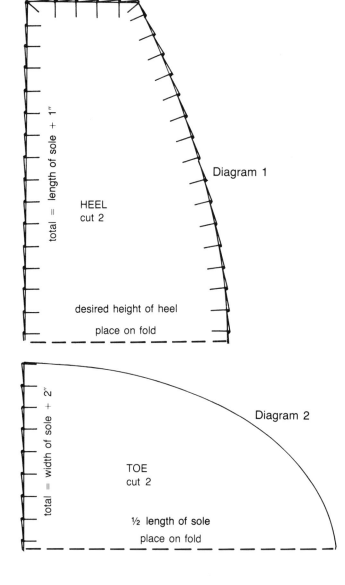

Diagram 1

total = length of sole + 1″

HEEL
cut 2

desired height of heel

place on fold

Diagram 2

total = width of sole + 2″

TOE
cut 2

½ length of sole

place on fold

Felt Tea Cozy

One side of the felt tea cozy shown in the photograph is plain, dark brown felt; on the other side, light-colored wool yarns were embedded during the felting process to form a random pattern. The yarn used to crochet the two sides together is the same as that used to form the pattern in the felt.

Materials
felt
wool yarn

Equipment
tape measure
paper pattern
scissors
crewel needle
crochet hook

Measure the length and height of your teapot, allowing for the fullness of the pot, as shown in Diagram 1. Using your measurements, cut a pattern to fit your teapot according to the dimensions given in Diagram 2. Cut two sides from your felt. Blanket stitch (Diagram 1, page 12) around the upper curved edges of each side as indicated on the pattern, making stitches random lengths if you desire.

Crochet the two sections together by working a single crochet stitch through the blanket stitch (Diagram 1, page 12), making as many rows of single crochet back and forth across the top as you desire.

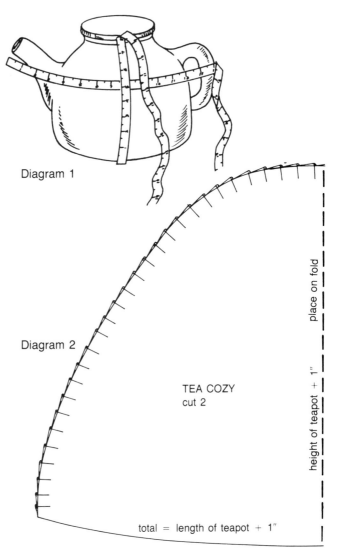

Diagram 1

Diagram 2

place on fold

height of teapot + 1"

TEA COZY
cut 2

total = length of teapot + 1"

Willow Table

Gypsies apparently originated the idea of willow furniture. It flourished during the Depression when out-of-work people shaped young saplings into furniture for sale. In the South today, you sometimes will see an old man unloading willow furniture from his pick-up truck, hoping to catch the eye of passersby. The chances are he won't be there tomorrow. It is, in many ways, still a gypsy art.

The old-timers complain they must go farther and farther away from home to find good "benders"—straight young willow branches no more than 2½" in diameter. They gather willow in the spring, "when the sap is up" and the branches are most pliable. When an old willow falls, it puts out long, slender suckers and rapidly generates a dense thicket of young saplings. It is these fallen trees that the furniture makers seek to harvest the second generation growth.

Florida swamp cypress is also used for furniture, but it must be gathered in small quantities and worked immediately because it loses its pliability as it dries. When the stringy bark is pulled away, cypress weathers to a beautiful silvery gray, and, like willow, it stands up to many years of outdoor use.

To bend willow into chairs with graceful arms and gently curving seats requires true practice and a lot of willow. But with only a dozen straight willow suckers, you can make a patio table in a few hours; the classic design can be used with any casual lawn furniture. The dimensions given here are for a dining height, but you can adjust the proportions to make an end table or cocktail table for your deck or patio.

Materials
willow, as straight as possible
- (A) 4 legs, 30" long, 1¼" to 1½" diameter
- (B) 4 side braces, 34" long, 1¼" to 1½" diameter
- (C) 4 diagonal braces, 50" long, ¾" to 1" diameter
- (D) 4 lower side braces, 32" long, 1" diameter (optional)

2" nails
3 pairs 72"-long leather shoe strings
36"-square glass top, at least ½" thick.

Equipment
saw
yardstick
pencil
hammer
scissors

Gather long saplings, cut away all small branches, and then cut the lengths needed from the straightest section of each sapling.

Use a yardstick to represent the 36″-square glass top. (Diagram 1.) Place two legs (A1 and A2) perpendicular to the yardstick so that each leg is 3″ from each end of the yardstick. In the finished table, the legs will be 3″ inside the glass top.

Place a side brace (B1) across the two legs, just below the top of the legs. Make sure that this horizontal piece does not overlap the yardstick at any point or it will prevent the glass top from resting evenly on the legs. Nail the side brace to the legs, using two nails at different angles for added stability. Repeat with two more legs and another side brace.

Have someone hold these two frames upright, 30″ apart and parallel to each other. Lay the yardstick across the two separate frames to make sure they do not bow outward more than 30″. Join the two parallel frames by placing another side brace (B3) inside the corners of each frame and nailing it to both the leg and the top side brace of each corner. (Diagram 1.) Repeat with another side brace (B4) on the opposite ends of the parallel frames.

While someone holds the basic table frame within a 30″ cube shape, nail in place four diagonal crossbraces (C). Beginning at one corner, nail a 50″ crossbrace to the leg just below the side braces (B). The brace should run diagonally across the table to the lower part of the opposite leg; nail the brace to the other leg about 8″ from the ground. Repeat with a diagonal brace from the top of each leg to the lower part of the opposite leg. These will cross in the center of the table as shown in the photograph.

If you do not plan to eat at the table, you can make it even more stable by nailing lower side braces (D) to the frame. These 32″ pieces should be fastened to the legs 8″ from the ground and parallel to the upper side braces (B). Although they do provide additional stability, the lower braces make it impossible to pull a chair up to the table while eating and were thus left off the dining table shown in the photograph.

At the turn of the century, the gypsies often used leather and wild vines as the only means of securing the joints, but it was quite a science to wrap vines tightly enough to do away with nails. We have used nails to ensure strong joints, but we have concealed the nails with leather string wrapped in a simple figure-eight pattern at each joint and where the diagonal braces cross each other in the center.

The beginning of the string is secured by wrapping consecutive rows on top of it. (Diagram 2.) To secure the end of the string, slide it through the center of the figure eight and pull it back under the consecutive loops, wedging it between the wood and the leather.

The upper corners are wrapped in two separate patterns, as shown in the diagrams. First wrap the top of the leg (A) to the end of the side brace (B2), supporting the upper side bar (B1) with this pattern. (Diagrams 2 and 3.) The second figure eight is made at the point where the diagonal brace (C) joins the leg near the top of the table. (Diagrams 3 and 4.) An additional wrapping conceals the nails at the point where the diagonal brace (C) is attached to the base of the leg. (Diagram 5.)

Position the glass on top of the willow frame.

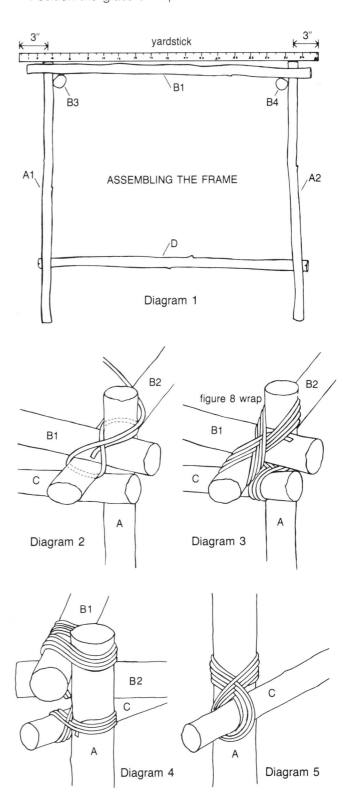

Twig Possum Home

In their first few months, wild creatures often survive only as long as their mother does. The most valuable help you can offer the orphans means the least contact possible. Ideally, you should protect the babies from danger without handling them, provide them with their accustomed diet, and return them quickly to their natural home. The naïve construction of a home of vines and cane allows the young creature to live outside but protected from larger animals. Once the animal has matured, the cane house becomes comfortable transportation into the deep woods, where the orphan will be set free.

Materials	Equipment
rough-sawn lumber	jig saw
young cane	garden shears
wild vines	pocket knife
leather shoe strings	drill with interchangeable
forked tree branch	bits
tacks	hammer

From rough-sawn lumber, cut two circles with a jig saw. One circle should be 8" in diameter for the top; the second, 13" in diameter for the base. Cut a forked branch from a tree to a length of about 20" and trim secondary twigs back close to the main branch. In the center of the top, drill a hole equal to the diameter of the branch. Wedge the branch through this hole, with the branch extending 2" above the top. Nail the other end of the branch to the center of the base from the underside. This branch will not only give your

construction more stability, but it will give the animal something on which to climb and scratch.

Cut a number of small canes to 18" lengths and cut two thicker vines or branches to 18". The larger vines or branches will frame the door and the cane will fill the sides. Drill two holes in the top and two in the base equal to the diameter of the larger vines and about 4" apart. Wedge the door frames in place.

Continue drilling holes in the top and base, about 1" apart and equal to the diameter of the small canes. Fit the 18"-long cane strips, one at a time, into a hole in the base and a corresponding hole in the top until canes fill the sides without gaps. Weave a thin honeysuckle vine around the home between the crossbars, leaving 2" of space between rows of vines.

Drill two holes in each of the upright door frames, one hole about 5" from the top and the second 4" from the base. (Diagram 1.) Make the holes one-half the diameter of the vines of the upright frame. From thick vines, cut two more pieces, each 4" long (or the distance between the upright frames). Whittle the ends of these pieces so that they will fit horizontally into the holes of the upright frames.

Before fitting these horizontal bars into place, however, drill small holes on the top of the upper bar, about 1" apart, and drill corresponding holes in the top wood circle. Drill small holes in the bottom of the lower bar and corresponding holes about 1" apart in the base. Fit the thick horizontal bars within the upright frames (Diagram 1), and fill in the space above and below with young cane strips.

Make a door by cutting two strips of thick vine, each 8" long. On one strip, drill holes about ½" apart and the diameter of the small cane; align the opposite strip and drill corresponding holes in it. Cut small cane into 4" strips and wedge into the corresponding holes. With leather shoe strings, hang the door from the upper bar as shown in the photograph; make a latch at the bottom of the door by bending a vine.

Finish the rough edges of the top and base by coiling a thin, flexible vine around the raw edges; tack the vine in place. In the extension of the branch above the top, drill three holes through horizontally and wrap a small vine through these holes to serve as a handle for carrying the animal back to the woods.

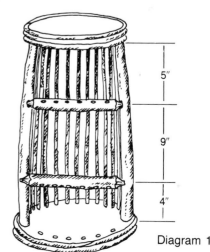

Diagram 1

Natural Pot Wraps

A handsome variety of planters can be made from the simplest natural materials—bunched twigs and dried stalks—wrapped around and glued to plain containers.

The container you cover should be large enough to hold a plant that is already potted. Good choices include institutional-size tin cans, plastic pots from nurseries, cardboard ice cream cartons with waterproof liners, or clay pots.

Almost any woody twig or branch—green or dry—can be used as a covering for the pots, but the straighter the twig, the easier it will be to handle. Small, pliant twigs are best; redbud and willow are especially good. Save your prunings from trees and shrubs or explore fields and marshes for grasses and reeds. The straight stalks of cattail, horsetail, broom sedge, faded daylilies, or other tall plants are good choices.

Materials
large container
black spray paint
twigs, grasses, or reeds
white household glue or waterproof glue
twine, wire, or heavy-duty thread
ribbon (optional)
protective spray (optional)

Equipment
pruning shears
large rubber bands

Spray the container black in case some of it should show through the natural materials.

Cut the plant material you have chosen about ½" longer than the height of your container. Place two large rubber bands around the container to hold the twigs in place while you work. Spread glue on a small portion of the container at a time. (Use a waterproof glue if your plant will be potted directly into the container.)

Add just a few twigs at a time. Small, straight ones will stick well to the glue, but irregularly shaped twigs may need to be wrapped in bunches with twine, wire, or heavy-duty thread to make them stay together. The wires can later be hidden by a band of long leaves or ribbon tied around the pot.

The wrapped pots are striking if left their natural color. But if you prefer a more finished effect, spray the pots with either a matte or a glossy protective spray.

Willow Basket

No matter how limited you consider your basket-making skills to be, you can easily construct a twig basket such as the one from willow shown above. The construction is elementary: branches of different lengths are nailed together in an inverted pyramid.

Materials

willow saplings, about 1¼" in diameter
1"- and 2"-long nails
3 willow shoots, each 3' long and ½" in diameter

Equipment

saw   ruler
miter box (optional)   hammer

Cut the willow saplings into sixteen pieces, four of each of the following lengths: 14", 12", 10", and 8" long (or corresponding lengths of different dimensions, depending on the size you wish your finished basket to be). Make the cuts on a 45° angle. The measurements given are from tip to tip; mark the length needed and then angle the saw toward the center of the stick as you cut.

The basket frame is constructed upside-down, as if you were building a pyramid. Place the four 14" pieces in a square, with the cut sides down and with the ends overlapping approximately 1½". Nail these pieces together.

Place the four 12" pieces on top, slightly inside the larger square; nail these in place. Repeat the nailing procedure with the 10" pieces, and then with the 8" pieces. Make sure the angled cuts are facing down.

Invert the pyramid and attach the handle to the lower sides. Tack one slim willow shoot to the 8" frame at the bottom of the basket. Loop it into a graceful arch and tack it to the opposite side of the 8" frame. Line up two more slim shoots on either side of the first and tack them to the center shoot. Nail all three shoots to the sides of the basket at each layer.

Antler Box

One day, if you are very, very lucky, you may find a deer antler while strolling through the woods. Deer shed their antlers in the late winter or early spring after the mating season is over. Antlers that are freshly shed are still dark in color; the longer they lie outdoors, the lighter the color. This tiny box was adapted from a colonial design for a shot container.

Materials

antler section
cork

Equipment

hack saw
vise
drill and drill bit
sanding disc
round sandpaper in coarse, medium, and fine
dark shoe polish or propane torch (optional)

Select the straightest section of the antler; this is often near the base. The base of the antler has a ridged texture while the tips tend to be smoother. With the hack saw, cut a section of antler in a length to equal the desired height of the container.

Clamp the section of antler in the vise. Choose a drill bit about the size you want the hollow of the container to be and drill out the center of the horn. Do not drill through the bottom of the container.

Change to the sanding disc on your drill. Starting with coarse sandpaper, sand the top and bottom edges of the container. Repeat with medium, then fine sandpaper until all scratches disappear. (Sand by hand if you find it easier.) You may wish to polish the sanded area with a hard felt wheel and jeweler's white rouge. (To darken a bleached antler, rub brown shoe polish onto the container or scorch the antler lightly with a propane torch.)

Place a cork in the top of the antler box.

Arm's-Length Baskets

An arm's-length basket is woven from materials within your arm's reach when you are sitting in one spot outdoors. The random mix of materials lends a casual style to the basket that is easy for an amateur to master. In just an hour or two, even a novice can carry away a basket full of private memories of a special afternoon.

To make a basket, you will need some long flat blades such as iris, yucca, palmetto, cornhusks, or daylilies to make the frame of the basket. To hold the frame securely, you will also need thin vines such as honeysuckle, wisteria, ivy, or small, flexible branches of weeping willow.

A third, filler material is a valuable complement to the structural materials. Choose a highly textured plant, such as Spanish moss or wild grass heads, which will help camouflage the weaving irregularities. No matter how closely you weave green materials, they will dry and shrink in a few days, contributing to the loose, casual feeling of these baskets. Because of the loose weaving, these are decorative and nostalgic baskets, important because of the place and time they were woven.

Materials

long, flat bladelike leaves (iris, yucca, daylilies, gladiola, cattails, palmetto)
thin, flexible vines (honeysuckle, wisteria, ivy, morning glory, willow branches)
filler material (Spanish moss, wild grasses, leaves, ferns)

Equipment

scissors

To make the bottom of the basket, weave the long, flat blades in an over-and-under lattice pattern. (Diagram 1.) To avoid a lopsided shape, alternate pointed ends with wide stem ends and make sure you have an equal number of horizontal and vertical blades. Keep adding one horizontal and one vertical blade until the latticed area is about the size you would like the finished basket to be.

Weave a double row of vines in a circle around the lattice pattern, defining the edge where the sides will turn up. To do this, make a fold in the vine about 12″ from one end and use the fold like a loop to secure the vine to one long blade, close to the lattice weave. Cross the vine to secure the loop and pull one length in front of the next blade and the other length behind the blade. Cross the vines again and continue weaving, securing each blade between the two vines. (Diagrams 2 and 3.)

Complete two full circles with the vines. The vine should be folded with uneven ends so that both vines will not run out at the same time. When one end runs out, fold another vine about 3″ or 4″ from its end.

Attach the fold, or loop, to the next blade and continue the same pattern as above. For several inches, you will be weaving with three vines; parallel the short end of the new vine with the longer vine already in place, treating the two vines as one.

Once the diameter of the basket is defined by a double circle of vines, begin to pull the blades up to shape the sides. The angle at which you hold the blades determines the shape of your basket. The long blades will act as the spokes, or frame, on which you weave the sides.

Use additional long blades as filler material on the sides, weaving them alternately in front of and in back of the upright spoke blades. Plants added for texture are also woven in the same manner. Follow each row of filler material with a double row of vines to hold the filler securely in place.

After a few rows have been woven on the sides, it will be necessary to add more spokes to maintain an even pattern. A long blade folded in half will work as two adjacent spokes. See Diagram 3 for how to insert these secondary spokes through the vine.

Continue weaving alternating rows of filler and vines until you are within 2″ of the end of the shortest spoke. (Always weave a double vine circle as the last, or top, row.) To finish the basket, trim all the spokes to 2″ above the last woven circle. Fold each trimmed end back inside the basket and weave it in and out of the finished rows. Trim any excess moss or protruding ends.

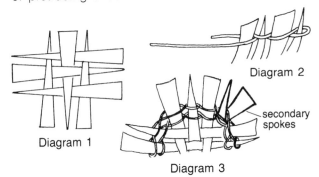

Diagram 1

Diagram 2

Diagram 3

secondary spokes

Birdhouse from a Hollow Log

Birds such as chickadees, bluebirds, and woodpeckers often seek a protected area inside a hollow tree or rotting fence post in which to build their nest. Thus, you can attract birds such as these to your property by providing a birdhouse made from a hollow tree. The bark covering and rustic appearance are enough to reassure even the shyest of birds.

Materials
hollow log, 7″ to 10″ in diameter
solid log, slightly larger than the hollow log
rough lumber board, ½″ to 1″ thick and still with bark
6-D galvanized finishing nails
3 galvanized wood screws

Equipment
chain saw
hand drill with 1½″ boring bit
hammer
screwdriver
ruler

If you live near a forest area which has been cut for commercial lumber, the hollow trees are easy to spot; they are the unwanted trees that are left standing. You'll also find hollow logs and rough boards in the scrap pile at the local sawmill or lumberyard.

From the hollow log, cut a section that is 12″ to 14″ long. Make one cut on a slant for the top of the birdhouse so that the roof will shed water. (Diagram 1.) Stand this section upright and make a vertical cut to remove one-quarter of the log from the higher side. (Diagram 2.)

From the solid log, cut two cross sections, each about 1″ thick, to be used as the roof and flooring of the birdhouse. (Diagram 3.)

Trim the piece of rough lumber so that it will fit inside the lengthwise cut in the hollow log and then trim the board to the same height as the hollow log. At least 6″ from the bottom of the board, drill a hole 1¼″ in diameter.

With the galvanized nails, attach the board (rough side facing out) to the lengthwise cut in the hollow log and secure the roof in place. Use the galvanized wood screws to attach the floor to the house. In this way, the floor can be removed for seasonal cleaning. (Diagram 4.)

Although the appearance of the birdhouse will be familiar to potential boarders, you can further put the birds at ease by hanging the house 5′ to 10′ from the ground.

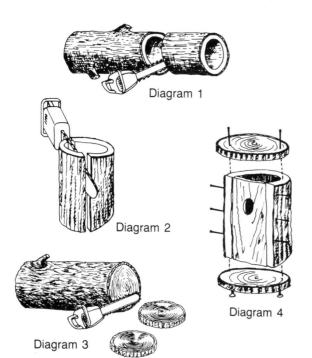

Diagram 1

Diagram 2

Diagram 3

Diagram 4

SummerCrafts

SEASHELLS: Jewels from the Sea

Chambered Nautilus

Lightning Whelk

Zigzag Scallop

The popularity of shells has fluctuated throughout history. The Greeks, striving for the "perfect order" exemplified in a scallop shell, incorporated the shell motif in classical architecture, and we duplicate their motifs in architectural detailing today. Victorian England revived the love of shells, and British seamen, in their sailors' valentines, gave us a precedent for shells in craft projects. With off-duty hours to while away on the ship, many sailors glued shells in intricate patterns on boxes as homecoming gifts for their wives or sweethearts.

Our mechanized society is experiencing a return to naturalism, and the popularity of shells has reached an all-time high as they

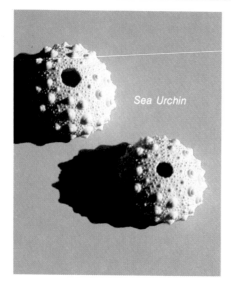

Sea Urchin

Juno's Volute

Lion's Paw

Scotch Bonnet

are valued both aesthetically and monetarily. Shells have always been brought home from beach vacations by the box full, and they are now as suitable in the living room as on the sunporch. Collectors display their shells side-by-side with the family cut glass.

In their enthusiasm for shells, clever decorators have invented uses for shells in every room in the house: a soap dish in the bathroom, a napkin ring on the table, and a night-light in the bedroom. Not only is the jewelry box covered with shells in a Victorian manner, but shells are inside, as well, on necklaces, barrettes, and pins.

FINDING SHELLS

The revived popularity of shells in the last decade has prompted a genuine concern about wasteful gathering of "live" shells—the term for shells in which the animal, a snail, is still living. With some shells already on the endangered list, an informal code has evolved among serious collectors; it is also a sensible guideline for the infrequent gatherers who want shells for craft projects.

The rule of thumb: don't go in the water. Pick up shells from the sand only. Those shells found in the tidal pools and mudflats of western Florida carry living snails, which must be left in their natural underwater home in order to survive and reproduce.

Part of the game of finding colorful shells on the beach is knowing *when* to look. Coastal storms throw many live shells up onto the beach. Once on the beach, the animals have been "sandblasted" until they cannot live, even if they were to be thrown back into the water.

Winter storms are especially fierce, providing good and environmentally safe harvesting of shells. (Storms also increase the number of shells in shallow water, but it is considered worse than unsporting to wade in after those survivors.) Pacific coast residents take note: it is unlawful to harvest any shell at any time from U.S.

True Tulip

Alphabet Cone

Spiny Jewel Box

beaches bordering the Pacific Ocean.

"Beach" shells are empty shells which are left when the animal dies naturally and are scattered on the sand in abundance as the tide goes out. These are the shells you will use most often for crafts projects.

Note: If you are land-bound, don't despair. See Suppliers, page 150, for commercial sources of seashells.

CLEANING SHELLS

Live shells washed up on the beach must still be emptied of their animal/owner. If you are planning a beach vacation to gather shells, reserve a place with a small kitchenette where you can clean the shells immediately. Otherwise, you may regret ever picking up the first shell. The small animals inside the shells begin to decay within a few hours, and their odor is proportionately much greater than the diminutive size of the animal itself.

There are several ways to remove the animal, depending on the amount of time you wish to spend and the size of the shell. If you are not in a hurry to work with the shells, the most efficient and the least objectionable method of cleaning for many people is referred to as "feeding the ants." Bury the shells under a layer of dirt or sand—near an ant hill, if possible. The ants will remove the animal for you. This method can

Bay Scallop

Nutmeg

Caribbean Land Snail

take as much as 4 weeks, however, which makes it impractical for vacationers.

Boiling is the most widely practiced method of ousting the animal. Boil small shells for 5 minutes; a conch shell, for about 30 minutes. Boiling kills the animal, but you must still pull it out of the shell using a crochet hook or tweezers and a firm, twisting motion. Make sure you get all of the animal out.

Some exhibiting collectors feel that boiling fades the more colorful shells, so they prefer to freeze the shells overnight. After allowing the shells to thaw for an hour or so, they then remove the animal with the crochet hook or tweezers.

For shells smaller than your thumbnail, the most suitable process is to soak the shells in an alcohol solution of 4 parts rubbing alcohol to 1 part water.

BLEACHING SHELLS

Bleaching is necessary only to completely remove any lingering odor or to loosen barnacles. Thin shells, such as olives and cowries, and deeply colored shells can, in fact, be damaged by bleaching.

For other shells that you wish to bleach, mix a half-and-half solution of chlorine bleach and water. Soak the shells in the solution

overnight. (Sand dollars may be soaked in a stronger solution to whiten their natural gray color.) If barnacles still adhere to the shell after soaking, scrape them away with a screwdriver or a nail file.

DRILLING SHELLS

With an electric drill and the smallest drill bit (1/16″ or 1/32″), you can drill holes in shells. Drill from the inside out and do not drill too close to the edge so you will not break the shell. Unless you have nerves of steel, put small shells in a vise before drilling.

Some shells are harder than others, as one collector said, "...just like some people's teeth are harder than others." The harder shells may become very hot while you are drilling. If so, drop the shell in a bowl of water until it cools.

An easy alternative method of making holes in seashells is to use a craft knife. Hold the craft knife in an upright position with the tip of the blade positioned at the point on the shell where you wish the hole to be. Twirl the craft knife, applying steady pressure, until the hole is cut through.

This method offers more control than you have with an electric drill, and the reduced pressure on the shell means that the shell is less likely to shatter.

GLUEING SHELLS

For shells that are too small or too hard to drill through, jewelers use a bell cap or an I-pin. A bell cap is simply glued on top of the shell so that the shell can be attached to a chain or cord. An I-pin can be bent to fit inside the shell but must be held in place with a generous application of glue.

Jewelry findings can be located through the yellow pages, and extra-strength adhesives prepared especially for shell projects are usually available through local craft shops. However, mail-order sources are also available for these supplies. (See Suppliers, page 150.)

POLISHING SHELLS

Many people apply a coating to restore the intensity of color that the shell has when wet. Serious collectors use baby oil thinned with lighter fluid (about 3 parts oil to 1 part fluid). More permanent coatings would disqualify a specimen shell from an exhibition. A coating of baby oil is not suitable, however, if you plan to use your shells for jewelry or inside a lamp.

Acrylic craft spray will prevent shells used outdoors from fading, and the spray will not darken the shells as shellac will. Shellac is particularly discoloring on sand dollars and other white shells.

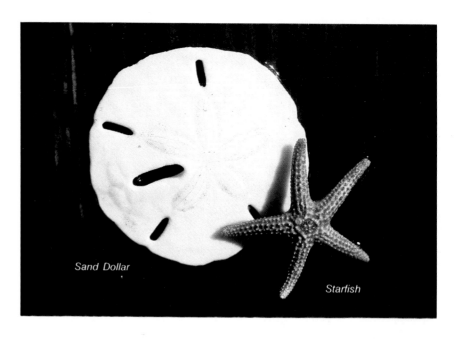

Sand Dollar

Starfish

Seashell Necklaces

What better way is there to delight in a rare or unusually formed shell than to suspend it about your neck? The design possibilities are as limitless as the colors and shapes of shells. Fasten a single shell on a simple silk cord or tie sliced shell segments at intervals along a cord. Suspend a shell with a coil of copper wire or combine crochet thread and brightly colored ribbon in a macramé pattern to complement a sliced nautilus.

Shells are lovely in combination with other materials, particularly with beads of pottery, glass, wood, or metal. Use 12-gauge jewelry wire to string shells and beads in a pattern that appeals to you; then attach a spring or barrel clasp to the ends of the wire.

through each hole and fold in half for a total of six strands of 24" extending from each hole.

Cut 10" of each color of ribbon and fold in half. Tie a small scrap of cord around these ribbons to hold them together at the fold. Tie this around all twelve cords on the right side and near the top of the shell.

*Using a 4" strip of coral ribbon, make a 1" wrap around all twelve cords on each side of the shell, as shown in the photograph.

Turn the shell around so that the cords are facing you. Work on the side with the ribbon streamers. Working on the macramé board with T-pins to secure the knots, number cords 1 to 12, left to right. Make 3 SK in each group with 1-4, 5-8, and 9-12.

Tie 4 SK with cords 3-6 and cords 7-10.

Using cords 5-8, tie 3 SK.

Nautilus & Ribbon Necklace

Materials
sliced nautilus shell
heavyweight ecru cotton crochet cord
½ yard (¼"-wide) coral satin ribbon
½ yard (¼"-wide) light blue satin ribbon
½ yard (¼"-wide) rust satin ribbon
white household glue
2 bell caps
barrel clasp
6 small seashells

Equipment
craft knife   transparent tape
scissors   T-pins
measuring tape   macramé board

TERMS AND ABBREVIATIONS
Wrap: Diagram 1.
Square knot: (SK) Diagram 2.
Diagonal double half hitch: (DHH) Diagram 3.
Vertical half hitch: (HH) Diagram 4.
Braid: Diagram 5.

Drill two holes in each side of the shell. The holes should be large enough for three strands of cotton crochet cord to fit through.

Cut twelve cords 48" long. Run three cords

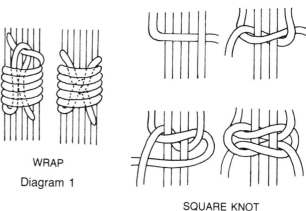

WRAP
Diagram 1

SQUARE KNOT
Diagram 2

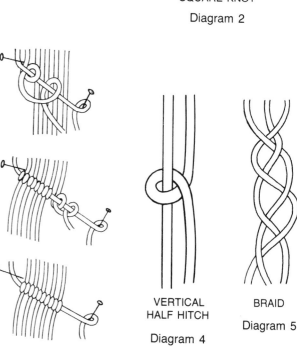

DIAGONAL DOUBLE HALF HITCH
Diagram 3

VERTICAL HALF HITCH
Diagram 4

BRAID
Diagram 5

Divide cords into two groups and number 1 to 6 and 7 to 12. With a 4" strip of blue ribbon, tie a 1" wrap around cords 1-6. Using a 4" strip of rust ribbon, tie a 1" wrap around cords 7-12.

Tie a SK in groups 1-4, 5-8, and 9-12. Make a SK in groups 3-6 and 7-10. Tie a SK with 5-8.

**Make a diagonal DHH with cords 1-6, left to right. With cords 7-12, make a diagonal DHH, right to left.

Renumber the cords 1 to 12. Tie 2 SK with 5-8. Repeat from ** twice.

Make a diagonal DHH with cords 1-6, left to right. With cords 7-12, make a diagonal DHH, right to left. Tie cord 6 to cord 7 with a vertical HH.

Divide cords into three groups, 1-4, 5-8, and 9-12, and braid. Make thirteen rows. Tape these together at the end of the row.

Repeat all steps from * with the cords on the right side of the shell.

Glue and crimp a bell cap to each taped end. Attach a barrel clasp to the bell caps.

Cut the ribbon streamers so that they stagger in length. Then glue a small shell to the end of each ribbon.

Shell & Brass Wire Necklace

Materials
18-gauge brass wire
scallop shell or similar distinctive seashell

Equipment
wire cutter
3/16"-diameter dowel
flat-nose jewelry pliers
hammer
anvil or other hard
  metal surface
electric drill

Cut two lengths of wire, each 6' long. Cut another length 3" long and a fourth 1½" long.

Coil one 6' length of wire around the dowel. To do this, begin by folding a ½" end of wire over the dowel. Carefully coil the wire evenly around the dowel, keeping the coils close together. (Diagram 1.) If the rows do not look even, use the pliers to push the rows together.

Coil the second 6' length in the same manner as the first. To shape the ends for the fastener, pull out 1" of one end of each coil and flatten the ends with a hammer on an anvil or other hard metal surface. (Diagram 2.)

To shape the opposite ends of each coil for the heart to hang the shell on, pull out 1" of coil and shape into a circular hook. (Diagram 3.) Flatten the circular end with a hammer.

Shape a 3" piece of wire into a heart shape, then flatten. (Diagram 4.)

Drill a hole in the top center of your shell according to the instructions in Drilling Shells (page 26). Insert a 1½" piece of wire through the shell and secure the ends together by twisting one end over and around the other.

Attach the heart shape to the shell hanger. Attach the circular ends of the wire coils to the heart shape from front to back so that the shell will lie flat.

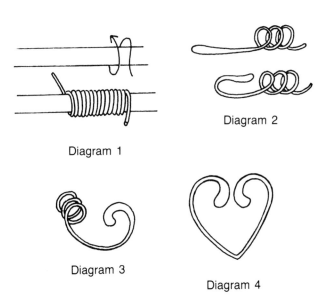

Diagram 1

Diagram 2

Diagram 3

Diagram 4

Shell Whimsies

A special touch can be added to the most ordinary of items with a single shell or a cluster of tiny shells. A stylish trio of shell stickpins is made by simply glueing a perfect little shell to a stickpin back. Haircombs are dressed up for summer with a little bit of satin ribbon and carefully chosen shells.

A dramatic mixture of shells can be effectively displayed in a glass ginger-jar lamp by simply turning the lamp upside down, removing the base, and filling it with your treasures from the seashore. Many small shells and pieces of coral would be just as striking as the mixture of larger shells shown here, and what better way is there to show off a handsome collection of shells?

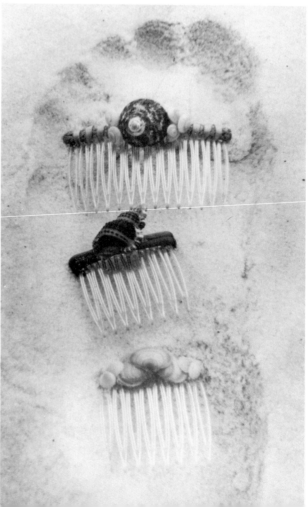

Shell Boudoir Mirror

A boudoir mirror from the five-and-dime store is elevated to special status with the addition of Atlantic jingle shells, one of the most plentiful of shells found along the high-tide line. This is an excellent project for children.

Materials
jingle shells
clear acrylic craft spray
mirror with metal or wood frame
527 Bond Cement
assorted miniature shells, about ¼" in diameter

Equipment
tweezers

Spray all the shells to be used with a clear acrylic craft spray.

Lay the mirror on a work table and pre-arrange fairly flat jingle shells on the edge of the frame, extending them over the edge so that they cover the frame. Remove the shells from the mirror one by one and lay them around the outside of the frame.

Hold a shell in one hand with tweezers, and with the other hand squeeze a little glue along the edges of the shell that will touch the frame and the mirror. Position the glued shell on the mirror frame and press lightly. Work around the frame, overlapping the shells until all shells are glued on. Let dry 24 hours.

Glue tiny shells between each two jingle shells to fill in the "V" spaces. Let dry 24 hours.

If the mirror has a stand or base, cover it with shells, starting with a row around the bottom edge and working up. Each row should slightly overlap the row below it. Let each row dry about 1 hour before adding the next row. Decorate with miniature shells.

Shell Tree Sculpture

Seashells are not the only bounty one finds when beachcombing. Bits of coral, sponge, and other undersea mysteries are often washed up. This sculpture utilizes some of those treasured bits and pieces. Worm coral forms the base, a coral sea whip makes the branches of the "tree," and coquina shells, which are very common on the coast of the Gulf of Mexico, make the "butterflies."

Materials
worm coral or driftwood
coral sea whip or sea fan
coquina shells and other small shells
527 Bond Cement
clear acrylic craft spray

Equipment
tweezers
hand or electric drill (optional)

Lay the coral or sea fan "tree" on a work table. Select a few colorful coquina shells and arrange them on the "tree." Pick up each coquina shell with tweezers, squeeze a small amount of glue onto the back of the shell, and press into place. When all have been glued in place, allow the arrangement to dry about ½ hour.

Find a hole or indentation on the worm coral or driftwood in which to "plant" your tree. If there is none, drill a hole with a hand or electric drill. Squeeze glue into the hole and press the base of the tree into the hole. Allow to dry. Glue a selection of small shells around the base of the tree.

Spray the entire arrangement lightly with clear acrylic craft spray. This will give it a fresh, "wet" look and help to keep it free of dust.

Shell-Encrusted Accent Pieces

If you have access to shells that winter storms deposit by barrelsful on the beach, you will appreciate the fact that these designs allow—even encourage—you to pile on more and more shells. A special richness results from the number, not the type, of shells used. Pieces of shell are worked in, as well as starfish, sand dollars, sea horses, and bits of coral—anything found on the beach. The finished projects display a further sophistication as a result of their being built on a three-dimensional form which permits the edges to be rounded instead of flat.

Table

Materials
hollow table, 18½" high and 13" square, constructed of ¼" plywood
clear epoxy glue
11"-square mirror
4 (¾" x 11¾") strips cut from ½" plywood
seashells
shellac
alcohol

Equipment
½"-wide paintbrush

Glue the mirror in the center of the table top. To get the raised effect around the top of the table, glue the ¾" x 11¾" plywood strips along each edge of the mirror. Precise alignment of the strips is not necessary because this area will be covered with shells after the sides of the table have been covered.

Working on a flat surface, position the table on its side and begin by putting glue on each shell and placing the shell on the wood, staying away from the raised top.

It is best to place most of the large shells in the first layer and the smaller shells on top and around them for the second layer. Put shells on in all directions, using different sizes to give the table an unplanned, natural look.

Cover the holes or spaces in the first layer of shells with a second layer of shells. In applying the second layer, turn some of the shells upside down or sideways to avoid a patterned look. As you work, you will notice that the corners are neatly covered by overlapping shells.

After finishing one side of the table, allow the glue to dry for at least 12 hours before turning the table to another side. All four sides of the table are covered with shells in the same manner. The more shells you use, the more attractive the table.

To finish the top of the table, glue shells on the edge of the mirror up onto the framing strips, having the shell partly on the mirror and partly on the strip. (Gaps between shells will be filled in later.) Work around all four sides of the mirror in this fashion. Then glue shells to the strips and over the sides of the table. After completing this, be as creative as you like with the second layer on the top of the table, using your favorite shells to fill in gaps in the first layer of shells.

Thin shellac with a small amount of alcohol and apply the shellac to the entire table, being very careful not to get any of the shellac on the mirror. (Avoid shellacking sand dollars because the shellac darkens them and destroys their natural beauty.)

Mirror

Materials
¼" plywood, 24½" × 8"
rectangular mirror, 19" × 5"
clear epoxy glue
2 (1" × 23½") strips cut from ½" plywood
1 (1" × 5") strip cut from ½" plywood
1 (3½" × 5") strip cut from ½" plywood
2 (¼" × 1") bolts with nuts and washers to fit
heavy wire used for hanging mirrors
seashells
shellac
alcohol

Equipment
electric drill with ¼" bit
½"-wide paintbrush

Glue the mirror to the piece of plywood, centering it between the long sides but leaving approximately 4″ of plywood exposed at the bottom. Glue a 1″ x 23½″ plywood strip along each side and the 1″ x 5″ strip across the top of the mirror, making sure the strips are not flush to the mirror. Glue the 3½″ x 5″ piece along the bottom of the mirror. Precise alignment of the strips is not necessary because this area will be covered with shells.

With an electric drill and ¼″ bit, drill a hole about 1″ from each corner of the top of the board. Fasten the bolts, washers, and nuts through these holes. Position the nuts on the front of the board so that any portion of the bolts that protrudes from the nuts will be covered by shells. Fasten hanging wire to the two bolts on the back of the board before tightening the bolts. (You must attach the bolts and the wire *before* covering the board with shells or many will be broken when you do secure the wire.) Make sure the mirror hangs correctly before proceeding. If it does not, adjust the location of the bolts until the mirror hangs properly.

Place the first layer of shells on the outer edge of the mirror by glueing them in a position where they touch the top of the wood strips and overlap the outside edge of backing board. Such overlapping will completely cover your frame from a side view. Position shells in a random pattern.

After completing the outer edge, begin the inside by glueing the shells so that they cover the edge of the mirror and the inside edge of plywood strips, having the shells partly on the mirror and partly on the strip.

Apply a second layer of "special" shells as described in finishing the top of the table. Shellac as directed for the table.

Wreath

Materials
1 ring cut from ¼″ plywood, 4½″ wide and 20″ in diameter to outside edge
1 ring cut from ½″ plywood, 3″ wide and 19¼″ in diameter to outside edge
2 (¼″ × 1″) bolts with nuts and washers to fit
heavy wire used for hanging mirrors
clear epoxy glue
seashells
shellac
alcohol

Equipment
electric drill with ¼″ bit
½″-wide paintbrush

Center the smaller wooden ring on top of the larger one and glue the pieces together. (For even more depth, you can cut four 1″-square spacers from ¼″ or ½″ plywood and glue them between the two rings. In this case, bolts longer than 1″ will be required. Generally, the larger the diameter of your wreath, the higher you will want to raise the smaller ring.)

Drill two holes for the bolts across the top of the ring so that the wire will not show through the center of the wreath. Secure the hanging wire to the bolts as directed for the mirror.

Glue shells all around the sides of the wreath, overlapping the outside edge so that the wreath is completely covered from a side view. After completing the outside edges, cover the inside edge in the same fashion. Finish the wreath with a second layer of smaller shells as described for the table.

Shellac as described for the table.

Seashells & Stained Glass

A panel of stained glass with shells worked into the design is an outstanding way in which to capitalize on the translucent quality of the seashells. The instructions given are applicable to stained glass panels of any design.

Materials
medium-weight paper for cutline drawing
poster paper for patterns
carbon paper
translucent seashells that will lie flat
stained glass (Use the pattern shown here to determine the amount of each color needed.)
¼"-wide copper foil
liquid soldering flux
household oil or kerosene
glass cleaner
60/40 or 50/50 solid-core wire solder
black patina
1"-thick strips juniper (red cedar)
white household glue

Equipment
scissors
masking tape
glass or wax marking pen
work board made of ½" plywood cut larger than intended panel
2 (1½"-long) thin wooden strips
glass cutter
grozing or fine-jawed pliers
fid or popsicle stick
hammer
horseshoe or glazing nails
small brush to apply flux
100-watt soldering iron with ⅜" chisel tip
router
glazing points

TERMS
Score: scratching the surface of the glass with a glass cutter.

Grozing pliers: glass pliers used to "chew" or grind away unwanted bits of glass.

Copper foil: adhesive-backed copper tape.

Fid: cone-shaped wooden tool used to adhere copper foil to glass.

Flux: chemical applied to copper foil areas prior to soldering.

Tack solder: melting a small amount of solder on foiled joints in order to hold glass in place prior to soldering.

Beading: to flow melted solder along copper foil lines, forming a smooth, high, rounded bead.

Patina: chemical that turns soldered lines black for an antique effect.

PREPARING THE PATTERN
Enlarge the pattern shown here or one of your design to the desired size on medium-weight paper. Leave the field (center) area of the pattern blank since this will vary with different shells. Center the shells and trace around them.

Make a line drawing for the cuts you will be making (cutline drawing). Mark placement lines for the solder between the shells and the border. If the field is divided, cutting of glass will be easier. Avoid exaggerated curved cuts.

After completing the pattern, transfer it to poster paper, using carbon paper. The patterns must be exactly the same. Cut out the poster-paper pattern. Check for accuracy against the cutline drawing. Number the pattern pieces and match the numbers on the cutline drawing.

Place tape on back of the pattern pieces and attach the patterns to the glass. Using a glass or wax marker, trace around each pattern piece.

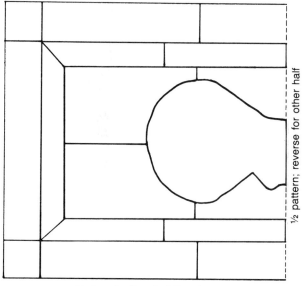

½ pattern; reverse for other half

Pattern for Seashell Panel

CUTTING THE GLASS
Prepare your workboard by placing your cutline drawing on it and nailing the two wooden strips at a 90-degree angle to act as a corner guideline.

Note: Always oil the glass cutter with household oil or kerosene before scoring a line. And always score the right side of the glass.

Starting ⅛" from the top edge of a piece of glass and exerting constant pressure, pull the cutter toward you. Stop the score ⅛" from the bottom edge of the glass. Never go over a score line twice.

To separate the glass, apply pressure beneath the score line. Straight lines may be separated in several ways: 1) place the score line along a table edge and quickly snap the glass in a downward motion; 2) tap along the underside of the score line to break the pieces apart; or 3) pull the two pieces apart with

grozing pliers by positioning the nose of the pliers just up to the score line and closer to one edge of glass and breaking down and away with the pliers.

Note: Because glass tends to break in straight lines, curved breaks are a bit more difficult to execute. To successfully score and break concave curves (there are several slight ones in this pattern), make several secondary straight-line scores leading into your primary curved score. Break each section of the curved cut carefully with the grozing pliers.

As you cut each piece of glass, position it on the cutline drawing.

APPLYING COPPER FOIL

Clean glass pieces thoroughly with glass cleaner to remove oil. Cut the copper foil in strips long enough to go completely around each piece and overlap ¼". Run the foil around the edge of the glass with an even amount of overhang on either side. Press the foil down onto the glass, folding the corners neatly.

Lay each piece flat; then, using a fid or popsicle stick, rub over the foil so that it adheres firmly to the glass on both sides. Apply copper foil to the shells in the same manner.

Position all foiled pieces of glass on the workboard and hammer nails around the perimeter to keep the glass from shifting.

SOLDERING THE DESIGN

With a brush, apply flux to all border joints on the front side of the design; tack solder these areas. Continue until you have tack soldered all joints on the front side. Apply flux to all the copper-foiled lines on the front side. With the soldering iron, run a thin layer of wire solder over all the lines.

After finishing the front side, repeat the soldering procedure on the back side.

Turn to the front side and build up a bead of solder on all soldered lines. This is done by running the soldering tip slowly along the lines while positioning the solder under the tip. The melting solder should flow along the lines leaving a smooth, raised bead. When raising a bead, always lift the soldering tip straight up when you reach a stopping point. This will keep the solder from running off the edge.

Note: Beading the solder on the back side of the window is optional. However, do make sure there are no small holes on the back side due to the reaction of the cool flux to the heat of the iron. Solder may have melted through to the back side. This should be spread along the soldered lines.

The same instructions apply to soldering around the shells. Any holes between glass and shells that are ¼" or smaller can easily be filled with solder.

Before cleaning the window, apply black patina to all soldered lines to darken them. After allowing the glass to cool, clean with warm, soapy water.

FRAMING THE PANEL

Stained-glass seashell panels may be framed in 1" juniper which has been routed out ¼" × ¼" to allow the glass to lie inside the lip. Corners should be mitered, glued, and nailed together. Finish wood as desired and secure the window in the frame with glazing points.

Seashell
Table Accessories

Seashell table accessories are a striking way to display unusually beautiful shells to their best advantage. Here, shells adorn napkin rings, fairly large specimens hold candles, and various smaller shells become budding "flowers." Each of these projects provides the opportunity for the shell to be closely examined, thus revealing the true beauty of nature's designs.

Flowers

Materials
16-gauge florist's wire
brown florist's tape
assorted shells
epoxy glue
brown eucalyptus

Equipment
needlenose pliers

Cut florist's wire to the desired lengths for "flower" stems. With florist's tape, wrap each length of wire completely. Glue a shell to one end of the wire with epoxy glue and allow to dry.

Note: With some shells, it may be necessary to shape the wire with pliers before glueing so that the wire fits more snugly inside the shell.

Measure down 2½" from the bottom of the shell and attach a eucalyptus leaf to the wire stem with florist's tape, wrapping the tape all the way to the bottom of the wire.

Candleholders

Materials
2 seashells with a deep cavity
resin and catalyst
candle cup holders
taper candles
epoxy glue

Equipment
mixing cups
mixing sticks
1½" × 2" cube-shaped resin mold

Make resin cubes according to directions on the can. After the resin has cured, remove from the molds. Glue shells to the resin cubes with epoxy glue and allow to dry.

With epoxy glue, fasten a candlestick cup holder to the inside of each shell and allow to dry. Light candle and drip a little wax into each cup holder; then set candles into the soft wax to hold them in place.

Napkin Holders

Materials
assorted shells
lucite rings
epoxy glue

Glue shell on top of lucite ring. Brace the ring in an upright position until the glue dries.

DRIED FLOWERS: Summer's Memories

The desire to preserve summer's blossoms for gray winter days is about as basic as the instinct to preserve food for winter. No one knows at what point a romantic pioneer adapted to flowers her commonsense methods of preserving herbs, corn, and other grains. But we do know that dried flowers were a common decoration in the eighteenth century.

Two hundred years later, subtle coloring and distinctive forms of summer plants are still treasured in winter homes. And with more drying processes from which to choose, we can now enjoy more color and a greater variety of materials all year long.

The drying process you use should be determined by the characteristics of the plant you wish to preserve and how you plan to use the plant after drying. Air drying—or hanging the plant upside down to dry—is fine for herbs that will be crushed for cooking and for strong-stemmed plants that will hold their shapes, such as yarrow, statice, and hydrangea. But if you want to keep the strong color and natural shape of delicate flowers for use in arrangements, you should cover the flowers with a drying medium such as silica gel. (The much-talked-about microwave drying is a simple way to speed up the silica gel process.)

Pressing, one of the oldest methods of preserving flowers, is still well suited to broad, flat foliage and to small flowers that will later be used for stationery or framed collages. Curing in a glycerin and water solution provides a means of drying foliage on the stem, but it works best with stiff leaves, such as magnolia and ivy. All of these methods are explained in greater detail in this section, and a partial list of those materials that respond best to each method is also given.

There are a few general groups of hard-to-dry plants; these are early spring flowers and plants with a high water content. The daffodils in the photograph were successfully dried in a microwave oven. However, people who live in humid climates will find that microwave-dried flowers do not last long as dried specimens because they tend to absorb moisture from the atmosphere more readily than do flowers dried by a more conventional method. If your attempts at drying do not work the first time, it may be just a matter of trying another drying method.

Keep in mind that whatever method you use to dry the plants, only flowers that are at their peak are worth preserving. Over-the-hill plants will disintegrate in a drying process. Plants are at their best early in the morning and should be clipped as soon as the dew has dried. During the flowering season, check the garden every day or so to pick new blossoms as soon as they open.

Always cut foliage for drying before the leaves begin to turn in the fall. By the time the weather turns cool, you can still gather some grasses and seedpods, but you should have flower blossoms and foliage already harvested and drying.

AIR DRYING

This is the least complicated and certainly the least expensive method of drying. Fortunately, it is also a very successful method of drying many plants. However, it does have its limitations: it will not hold true color in summer blossoms, and delicate plants will lose their shape. Rely on air drying for plants with firm, woody structures, for herbs that will be crushed for cooking, and for scented flowers in potpourri.

Although you sometimes hear of a happy accident when someone left a summer arrangement in the vase and the plants dried standing upright, that is a rare case. (Hydrangeas are the exception. They do dry best in a little water.) Most plants should be stripped of foliage and hung upside down in a dark, dry spot—dark to retain as much natural color as possible, and dry to prevent the plants from rotting. A spacious closet or attic is ideal because you need enough room to hang the plants without crowding; the more air space surrounding the plants, the quicker they will dry. In the Lower South, air circulation is particularly important to prevent rotting or mildew.

Strip the leaves off the stems and tie the plants in small bunches for hanging. Because the stems shrink as they dry, plants often fall out of bunches tied with string; tiny, freezer-bag rubber bands are better since they will shrink with the drying stems and keep the plants from falling.

Air drying, although an ancient practice, is still the most popular process for preserving herbs; see Dried Herbs, page 50.

DRYING MEDIUMS

This is the favorite method of those who want flowers for dried arrangements because a drying medium preserves the color and the shape of even delicate petals. Flowers are buried in a highly absorbent material—a commercial silica gel, a mixture of borax and cornmeal (1 part borax to 5 parts cornmeal), or in clean, very dry sand—which sifts between the petals to remove moisture.

Silica gel, which is available at drug stores and some florists, may seem expensive, but it can be used many times if it is dried out in a low-temperature oven and stored in an airtight container after each use. Although less expensive initially, drying with the borax and cornmeal mixture or the sand offers less predictable results. (Non-green cat litter is also often used as a drying medium.) The borax and cornmeal mixture clings to the petals, leaving an unsightly white coating. Since you cannot be rough with dried flowers, you must gently brush the powder away with a small artist's brush. Most who experiment with other mediums return to silica gel as the method that is the least time-consuming and yet produces the most consistently satisfactory results.

Although flowers can be dried with the stems on (strip the leaves and dry them separately), this requires more and longer boxes to accommodate the flowers, which should not touch each other while drying. It is better to leave only a ½" stem on the blossoms so that many more will fit into one box. After the blossoms are dry, flexible stems of florist's wire can be added along with the dried leaves.

Cover the bottom of a shoe box or a larger, shallow box with about ½" silica gel. Place the flowers face down, with space between each flower, and gently sift more silica gel between the petals and around each flower until the flowers are completely covered. Do not cover the box itself or the moisture cannot evaporate from the drying medium.

One word of caution to those using this method of drying: flowers left in the medium too long will become brittle and fall apart. A rule of thumb is that the thicker the petal or the larger the blossom, the longer it will take to dry. As an example, pansies will dry in about 4 days, but zinnias or large roses will take 10 days to 2 weeks. As with all drying methods, rainy, cool weather or confined drying space will pro-

long the process. The safest method is to test a few blossoms every day or so and rebury those that are not yet dry.

When the blossoms are dry, use a small, soft brush to clean away any grains of the drying medium. Cut florist's wire in lengths for a well-proportioned arrangement. Push one end of each wire crosswise through the base of a flower and twist the end back around the longer wire stem. Wrap florist's tape firmly around the base and wire and continue wrapping the tape down the full length of the wire stem. Some flowers with small bases may also require glue to hold the wire.

Microwave Drying

If you have a microwave oven, you can speed the drying process from 2 weeks to 2 minutes. Be sure to check with the manufacturer of your oven first. Some manufacturers have encountered damage to the microwave unit during drying processes and, therefore, will not honor the warranty once flowers have been dried in the oven. In contrast, at least one manufacturer has published its own book on drying flowers in the microwave. To be sure of the capabilities of your oven model, write or call the number given in the owner's manual.

The procedure is the same as outlined above for drying in a medium, except that you must use a glass casserole for the silica gel and flower heads. A glass or ceramic cup filled with water must also be in the oven during the drying process. Complete instructions for drying flowers in a microwave appear on page 41.

PRESSING

A very old and inexpensive method, pressing is best suited to ferns, small leaves, cornhusks, and flowers to be flattened for use in framed collages or handmade paper (page 61). With a damp cloth, wipe away dust and place the leaves in a book between layers of paper towels. Use waxed paper between the pages of the book and the paper towels to prevent stain; then weight with heavy books for 2 weeks.

GLYCERIN CURING

Magnolia leaves in holiday decorations are the best known example of glycerin-cured leaves, but a great variety of summer greens could also be preserved with this method. Elaeagnus, wax leaf ligustrum, loquat, and other similar leaves that have a firm structure will preserve well in a glycerin solution.

When you collect branches of foliage, slit about 2″ of the stem ends to increase the absorption of the glycerin solution. Stand the branches in a solution of 1 part glycerin to 2 parts water for 1 to 3 weeks, depending on how much color change you want. After a week of processing, you may substitute water during the second week for a lighter, more natural color. If you want a darker, bronzelike tone, leave the branches in the glycerin solution for several weeks.

Because glycerin is expensive, some people opt for a solution of equal parts permanent antifreeze and water to cure foliage. This is a quicker but less reliable process because it cannot provide uniform color and often makes leaves too brittle to handle.

MATCHING THE PROCESS TO THE PLANT

The condition and the maturity of the plant when it is picked (which you can selectively control) and the weather affect your success with dried materials. Always dry more than you think you will need.

The following lists of plants suited to each drying process are by no means complete; they are offered to get you started with successful drying of local plant materials.

Air Drying
Artemisia
Baby's Breath
Cattails
Celosia
Chinese Lantern
Cockscomb
Crepe Myrtle Seed Heads
Deer's Tongue
Dock
Dusty Miller
Golden Rod
Herbs (all varieties)
Hydrangea
Knotweed
Lunaria (Honesty or Money Plant)
Onion Flower
Okra Pods
Pampas Grass
Princess Feather
Rabbit Tobacco
Rose Hips
Statice
Strawflower
Sumac
Tansy
Thistle
Wild Grasses
Yarrow

Glycerin Curing—Foliage
Aspidistra
Beech
Boxwood
Cleyera
Elaeagnus
Eucalyptus
Holly
Ivy
Laurel
Ligustrum
Loquat
Magnolia
Oak
Pittosporum
Rhododendron
Sweet Gum
Tea Olive

Drying Mediums
Ageratum
Anemones
Balloon Flower
Butterfly Weed
Candytuft
Chrysanthemum
Hybrid Clematis
Columbine
Cosmos
Cornflower
Dahlia
Daisy
Delphinium
Geranium
Hibiscus
Hydrangea
Hollyhock
Larkspur
Lilac
Marigolds
Peony
Pinks
Poppy
Queen Anne's Lace
Ragged Robin
Roses
Snapdragon
Stock
Sweet Pea
Zinnia

Pressing
Acacia
Coleus
Ferns
Forget-Me-Not
Geranium Leaves
Gingko Leaves
Pansy
Violets

Microwave-Dried Flowers

Materials
fresh flowers
silica gel
florist's wire
green florist's tape
white household glue
  (optional)

Equipment
scissors
flat, glass casserole
microwave oven
coffee cup
small, soft paintbrush

Note: Use any glass, paper, or oven-proof dish. Never use metal in a microwave oven.

Choose flowers bright in color, very fresh, half-open, firm, and with thick petals. It is best not to use flowers that are fuzzy because the silica gel sticks to the petals and makes it difficult to remove the grains.

Cut flowers, leaving ½" stems. (Leaves should be dried separately and added later to the stems of the flowers with florist's tape.)

Because timing will vary with different flowers, it is best to process flowers of about the same size and type in one casserole, repeating the process for each flower type.

Pour a layer of silica gel into the glass casserole. Place the flowers on top of the silica gel, making sure they do not touch each other. Sprinkle silica gel evenly over the flowers, making sure all spaces between the petals are filled. Cover the flowers completely; no part of the petals should be exposed to the air.

Place a coffee cup filled with water in the corner of the microwave oven. Place the flowers in the oven and heat for 2 to 3 minutes.

Remove the flowers and allow them to cool for 15 to 20 minutes. If the base still has moisture trapped in it, bury only the base again in silica gel and return it to the oven for 1 minute. Be sure to put the cup of water in the oven each time.

Carefully remove the flowers from the silica gel. Use a soft paintbrush to remove all the grains.

When the flowers are completely dry and cool, attach a stem of florist's wire as explained on page 39. Wrap the entire length of the wire stems with florist's tape.

Roses

The sweet, summer fragrance of roses is easily preserved in perfumes and potpourri. A rose bead necklace carries its perfume for months, revived by the warmth of body heat when it is worn.

In some of the new hybrid roses, fragrance has been sacrificed for color or prolific blooming, so the best roses to use for these projects are often the old-fashioned standbys such as *rosa centifolia*, the cabbage rose; *rosa gallica*, the French rose; and *rosa damascena*, the damask rose.

Use the most fragrant roses you can find and pick them in early morning on a sunny, warm day. At that hour, and in newly opened roses, the fragrant oils are most concentrated.

Rose Bead Necklaces

Traditionally, rose beads were strung into rosaries. As each bead was counted in prayer, the warmth of the worshiper's hand intensified the fragrance of the beads. Even outside the Catholic church, a rose bead necklace often held great sentimental value because it was made of roses from grandmother's garden or from a bride's bouquet. Delicately colored and scented, a rose bead necklace is a romantic accessory still.

Materials
rose petals
powdered orrisroot
acacia powder (also known as gum arabic)
rose oil (or unscented vegetable oil)
quick-dried rose petals (optional)
clear filament (fishing line)
jewelry findings (fasteners)

Equipment
carbon steel knife (optional)
cast-iron pot (optional)
double boiler
wooden spoon
waxed paper
sewing needle

MAKING THE "DOUGH"
As rose petals harden into beads, they usually take on shadings of soft pastels, but it is possible to make coal black beads. Alternative instructions for making black beads are given in parentheses.

Remove the hard, white "nail" from the base of

each petal and tear the petals into small pieces of equal size. (For black beads, cut the petals with a carbon steel knife.)

To each cup of torn petals, add ½ teaspoon powdered orrisroot and at least 2 tablespoons acacia powder. Mix well with your fingers and transfer the mixture to a double boiler (cook black beads in a cast-iron pot). Over medium heat, cook and stir the petals until you see the oils begin to seep out. Remove from heat and knead the petals with your fingertips to make a stiff dough. Squeeze the dough to wring out excess moisture and reserve this "glaze" for later use.

FORMING THE BEADS

Lubricate your hands with rose oil or an unscented vegetable oil. Pinch off about ⅛ teaspoon of the dough and roll it between your palms to form a bead. Repeat until all the dough has been used. The beads will shrink as they dry, so make them slightly larger than you wish for your necklace.

Dry the beads on waxed paper. After 24 hours, turn the beads, reshape if necessary, and continue drying until very hard.

GLAZING THE BEADS

With the glaze left over from cooking the petals, dip or brush a surface coat over each bead to polish and further harden the beads. If you are pleased with the color of the beads at this point, let the glaze dry and rub them with rose oil for extra protection against moisture before stringing.

RESTORING COLOR

If you feel that the beads have faded too much, you can add fresh color on the surface of the beads with quick-dried petals. Place new petals on a cookie sheet that is covered with paper towels. Heat the petals in a barely warm (110°F) oven until they are crisp and dry. Leave the oven door ajar to speed the evaporation of the moisture. (Store dried petals in an airtight container if not used immediately because they will reabsorb moisture from the air.)

Coat one bead at a time with glaze. While the glaze is still wet, wrap one large, unblemished, dry petal around the bead. Roll the bead between oiled palms to smooth the petal, and recoat the bead with glaze.

An alternative method of covering the bead for better color is to crush the dried petals, then to roll the beads first in the glaze, then in the crushed petals. Allow to dry for 10 minutes. Roll the bead between oiled palms, press the petals into the glaze, let dry, and recoat with glaze.

STRINGING THE BEADS

Puncture the beads with a sewing needle and string them onto clear filament. Tie jewelry fasteners onto each end of the filament.

If the fragrance fades over several months, it can be renewed by rubbing the beads with rose oil.

Rose Oil

Rose oil can be used as your personal perfume or in an oil-burning lamp to scent an entire room. Home-made candles and soaps are also enhanced by its sweet, light fragrance, and a dab of rose oil will revive your rose bead necklace for many months.

The instructions given here apply to perfumes made from other fragrant flowers as well as roses. Try making a collection of perfumed oils.

Materials
fresh rose petals
safflower or other unscented vegetable oil

Equipment
glass, enamel, or ceramic container
strainer

Fill the container half-full with oil and pack fresh rose petals in layers until the container is tightly filled. Cover the container and set aside for 48 hours.

Press the oils from the petals in a strainer, preserving the oil and discarding the petals.

Pack fresh petals again into the same oil and set aside for 48 hours. Repeat this cycle several times, using fresh petals each time, until the oil absorbs a concentrated fragrance.

Strain the oil a final time and store it in a dark, airtight bottle.

Rose Water

Rose water is a delicate perfume, less concentrated than rose oil. Apply to pulse points as you would any perfume or luxuriate in a hot bath scented with rose water. Rose water from organic gardens may be used in cooking, but it is not safe if commercial insecticides have been used on the rose bushes.

Materials
fresh rose petals
water

Equipment
glass, enamel, or ceramic container
strainer

Fill the container with tightly packed rose petals and cover the petals with water. Cover the container and leave it in a sunny window for at least 48 hours. Strain the petals from the now-fragrant water. Store rose water in the refrigerator in a dark, airtight container.

Potpourri

Potpourri allows you great freedom in the combination of materials; you can experiment with any of the ingredients, substituting your garden flowers for those ingredients used in the potpourri recipe given here.

In adapting a potpourri recipe, keep in mind that three basic categories must be combined for a successful mixture: a base of fragrant flowers and spices, a fixative to preserve the fragrance, and oils to intensify the fragrance. You may wish to include other dried flowers for more color and for more variety of texture, but a potpourri can be as simple as rose petals mixed with a few spices, oils, and a fixative.

Decorative jars or sachets of potpourri make thoughtful, fragrant gifts any time of the year.

FLOWERS

Rose petals and rosebuds are the most popular base for potpourri because their fragrance can be preserved in drying. Other good choices are petals from other fragrant flowers such as magnolia, honeysuckle, jasmine, stock, sweet pea, and violets.

To retain the maximum fragrance, dry these flower petals slowly, away from sunlight or intense heat. Spread a single layer of buds and petals on paper towels or screens and leave in a well-ventilated spot. Turn the petals every day or so until they are "cornflake" dry. In cool or humid weather, drying may take up to 2 weeks.

SPICES

Whenever possible, use whole spices. They will distribute evenly in the mixture while powdered spices tend to sift to the bottom of the container.

The more exotic spices listed here may be omitted, or they can be ordered from the sources given in Suppliers, page 150.

FIXATIVES

Orrisroot, the strongest fixative, is difficult to find, unfortunately. Powdered orrisroot, often found in pharmacies, is more common than the Florentine cut root, which, although more effective, must be ordered. Gum arabic, found in health food stores and pharmacies, is more widely available and may be substituted for orrisroot.

OILS

Oils provide the volatile release of the fragrance and should be included in the first mixing of the potpourri and used again after several months to refresh the fragrances. (Brandy may also be sprinkled on to refresh old potpourri.)

TIMING AND ADJUSTING

Toss the three basic ingredients together in a large bowl along with any additional dried flowers or herbs which may add color. Cover the container and allow to stand for 1 or 2 weeks. At first, the mixture will smell rather sharp and raw, but it will mellow gradually. Test it every few days and adjust the fragrance by adding oils, if needed.

INGREDIENTS
Flowers and Spices
3 cups dried rosebuds
3 cups dried lavender blossoms
¼ cup whole cloves
¼ cup cinnamon sticks, broken into small pieces
¼ cup whole allspice
¼ cup blades of mace (optional)
¼ cup Frankincense tears
1 teaspoon salt (to absorb moisture)

Fixatives
10 crushed tonka beans
1 cup orrisroot (preferably Florentine cut)

Oils
⅛ ounce cinnamon oil
⅛ ounce lemon oil
¼ ounce rose oil
¼ ounce tincture of musk (You can make your own by mixing 1 part musk oil to 10 parts grain alcohol or vodka; let stand for 3 weeks.)

Flowers for Color and Texture (optional)
Blue malva
Everlastings
Hollyhocks
Rose petals
Orange blossoms

Passion Flower Dolls

A child's imagination often sees the exotic and mysterious in things adults may take for granted. Thus the feathery purple blossoms of the Passion Flower, or May Pop, become glamorous dancers with costumes worthy of a Busby Berkeley production.

When the wild vines are in bloom during July and August in the South, a romantic little girl can have not just one doll, but a chorus line to entertain her for an afternoon.

The Latin dancers come to life when selected stamen are removed, leaving two arms. The lead dancers here have an elaborate headdress of three stamen, but the chorus line performs without headdresses.

By trimming away the feathery purple edges, an upside-down blossom may also become a male dancer with an oversized Mexican sombrero, as shown in the diagram.

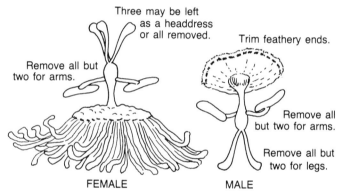

Three may be left as a headdress or all removed.

Remove all but two for arms.

Trim feathery ends.

Remove all but two for arms.

Remove all but two for legs.

FEMALE   MALE

Clover Chains

Remember trying to jump rope with a clover chain? Tying chains is still a consuming pastime for children from May to September. And although the delicate clover chains do not work very well as a jump rope, they make wonderful jewelry for a doll and her mother. They can also turn a swing or garden chair into a fantasy land; or tie a chain between two trees and race with the fairies to see who will break through the finish line first.

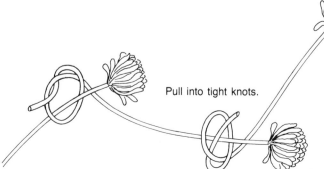

Pull into tight knots.

Cane Pipes

Many of us had a bamboo whistle in our childhood and remember it with great fondness. Why not take the basic principle, expand it a bit, and make a bamboo flute, better known as the "Pipes of Pan," named for that impish creature of mythology?

Materials
cane
cotton crochet thread
white household glue or electric glue gun with glue sticks

Equipment
hand saw
hand or electric drill with auger bit or a metal skewer
knife

Select four or five stalks of dried cane that are ⅝" in diameter at the base. These should be straight and unbranched. Remove the leaves. With the hand saw, cut twenty-six pipes from three canes, graduating the length of the pipes from 10" to 2½". After cutting the 10" pipe from the longest cane, cut each successive pipe about ⅜" shorter than the preceding pipe. The diameters of the pipes should decrease with the length.

Test and correct the pitch of each pipe. To do this, hold the pipe in a vertical position and blow forcefully down the tube, changing the angle slightly until you hear a clear note. To raise the pitch, saw a small length from the top of the pipe. To lower the pitch on a pipe with two or more nodes, bore through one of the nodes. This may be done by using a power drill with an auger bit or by burning a hole with a heated metal skewer.

Arrange pipes side by side on a flat surface in graduated lengths as shown in the photograph. Cut a piece of cane 1" longer than the combined width of the pipes. Split the cane lengthwise with a sharp knife. With an electric glue gun or white household glue, attach one-half of the crosspiece parallel to and 1" below the top edge of the pipes. When the glue has dried, glue the other crosspiece to the opposite side of the pipes, aligned with the first crosspiece. Allow the glue to dry completely.

Using cotton crochet thread, lash the crosspieces in place by passing the thread between successive pipes and around the crosspieces. Cut a second crosspiece 2" longer than the first. Split the halves and glue at an angle along both sides of the bottom of the pipes, as shown in the photograph. Allow to dry; then lash to secure.

Sandcast Lamps

Bring home the impressions of your summer vacation in the form of sand castings, and the memories will linger throughout the year.

Pushing the sand around at the beach has fascinated children for hours on end, and a sand casting gives them something to take home—a permanence that defies the incoming tide. Children are masters of their own designs, using fingers and toes and shells and stones to scoop out shapes in the damp sand. Casting a lamp base will draw adults into the act.

The basic instructions given here will apply to any sand-casting project. Although the lamp base must be poured in two identical halves, most projects can be completed with one casting. The lamp base is easy to make if you use a mold, such as a large bottle, to make the impressions in the sand. But if you have held onto the bravado of childhood and choose to create your own shapes freehand, keep in mind that the lamp will require a broad base and a balanced mass in order for it to stand upright.

Plan to spend some time taking a swim or doing something else between "halves" because the entire project will take about 3 hours to complete.

Materials
15″ threaded rod (⅜″ diameter)
sand
10 pounds No. 1 casting plaster or white art plaster
1 lamp kit including 8′ feet of cord, socket clip-on, plug, and harp

1 square felt
white household glue
lamp shade

Equipment
large bottle or container	plastic cottage cheese
hacksaw	container
plastic bucket	pliers
wooden paint stirrer	scissors

Note: If you do not live near a beach, get a bucket of sand and a large aluminum foil roasting pan. Add enough water to the bucket of sand to make it moist. Then transfer the sand to the roasting pan. This will be your "indoor beach" or sandbox. At the beach it is advisable to have a source for fresh water.

PREPARING THE MOLD
Select an empty bottle for its shape before you go to the beach. With the hacksaw, cut the threaded rod 1″ longer than the height of the bottle. If you are planning a free-form lamp, cut the rod to the desired length. A small lamp would be about 11″ high and a large lamp about 15″ high. If you already have the shade, the lamp base should be a couple of inches taller than the depth of the shade.

Scoop out a hollow in the damp sand. Lay the bottle in the sand and mound more damp sand up around the sides so that half of the bottle is buried. Press firmly on the bottle and pack the sand surrounding it. Carefully lift the bottle from the sand. If you are doing a free-form shape, make the mold even on each side with a flat base so that the lamp will stand straight. Make a small mound at the center of the base. This is where the threaded rod will protrude from the plaster.

Add texture and design to the impression in the sand by using your fingers, shells, sticks, etc. Remember: everything will come out in reverse on the plaster casting.

MIXING THE PLASTER
Pour approximately 6 cups of water into the bucket. Add about 7 cups of plaster to the water and stir with the paint stirrer until the mixture is smooth. (If you are working indoors, do not mix plaster in the sink or let any go down the drain.) Wait a few minutes to allow the plaster to become the consistency of heavy cream. Use the plastic container to ladle the plaster into the sand mold. Pour the plaster gently so that you do not disturb the design. Fill the mold up to the top edge with plaster.

While the plaster is still wet, lay the threaded rod lengthwise in the plaster, resting each end on the sand rim. Be sure that no plaster gets into the open ends of the rod.

Allow the plaster to harden. It will feel warm to the touch as it sets; it is ready to handle when it feels cool. Allow any excess plaster to harden in the plastic bucket. When it has set, bend the plastic side of the bucket and pop the hardened plaster out. Throw it in the trash can and clean up any scraps of plaster left on the beach. Cleanup is surprisingly easy after the plaster has hardened.

Carefully lift the plaster casting from the sand mold and rinse it off. If you are working indoors, put it in a dishpan so that the loose sand will not clog the sink drain. After the sand has settled to the bottom of the pan, you can pour off the water and discard the sand in the trash.

MAKING THE SECOND HALF

Make a second impression in the sand with the bottle. Decorate it just as you did the first half. If your design is free-form, bury the first half in the sand to get the right size and shape. Follow the steps given above for mixing the plaster.

After you have poured the plaster into the second mold, let it harden slightly and then gently lay the first half on top of the soft plaster of the second half. Line up the edges before you let the halves touch; once they are together, they are stuck permanently. Pile sand up over the side seams all the way around and let it set for an hour.

Dig the lamp out of the sand and rinse it off. If the seam cracks, make a mixture of wet plaster and sand and apply it to the crack with your fingers. Cover the seam with sand and allow the plaster to harden; then rinse.

Set the lamp base on end to see if it will stand properly. If it is lopsided, scrape away some of the plaster with a knife to make the base even. If it is very bumpy on the bottom, you may want to even it off with sandpaper, a fine-tooth saw or a hacksaw. At this stage, the plaster will still be soft and easy to cut through. Cut a small notch in the base for the cord to pass under the lamp.

Leave your sand casting in the sun or a warm, dry place for about a week to "cure." This may take longer, depending on the thickness of the plaster and the humidity.

After the casting is cured and dry, spray it with a clear acrylic spray coating. This will keep it from shedding sand and will preserve the surface. Sand castings do not always need to be coated, but if you are planning to keep the casting in your home, the loose sand can be a nuisance.

WIRING THE LAMP

Pass cord through the threaded rod. Attach the slipneck to the rod and the base of the harp; add a knurled nut to hold it in place. Wire the cord to the socket. Attach the harp to the top of the lamp. (Screw-on harps that screw onto the socket itself are also available.) Attach the plug to the other end. (Most lamp kits have instructions on the package.)

Cut a piece of felt to fit the base of your lamp. Glue the felt to the base with white household glue to prevent the lamp from scratching the surface of your table. Add the shade and the lamp is complete.

DRIED HERBS: The Taste of Summer

Although drying herbs and flowers is often associated with crisp fall days, herbs are more productive if they are clipped and dried all summer long. Cutting herbs back when they bloom will encourage second growth and double your harvest.

Most herbs should be cut just before their blossoms open to retain the peak of flavor and fragrance. There are two exceptions, however—chives and dill. It is a shame to miss the delicate lavender blossoms of chives, so you may want to enjoy their full bloom and cut them just as the flowers begin to fade.

Unlike most other herbs, which are prolific, dill will produce only one crop each season. It should still be harvested just as its flowers begin to open, but leave several plants to go to seed. Dill that grows from natural seeding in the garden will produce stronger plants in the second season. To enjoy dill all summer, stagger spring plantings in two-week intervals.

Herbs mature at varying times, so from August until frost, make it a habit to check your herb garden once a week. Clipping at mid-morning on a sunny day also helps guarantee maximum flavor. Annuals (parsley, dill, basil) can be cut back to within 3" or 4" of the ground. But to insure second growth, perennials (thyme, tarragon, chives, rosemary, oregano) should not be cut more than two-thirds of the way down the stalk. Perennials, particularly, benefit from summer harvesting. If they are cut back drastically in the fall, an early frost can kill the plant.

Rinse garden dust off the herb leaves under a light stream of running water. Then wrap several stems together with a small rubber band. (The stems will shrink as they dry and will fall out of string ties.)

Optimum drying conditions are found in a cool, dry, and dark place, such as a pantry or closet. Although racks of drying herbs in a kitchen have a marvelous visual appeal, some flavor is sacrificed in daylight. You might dry summer herbs in a closet and hang the last fall harvest in the kitchen.

Many experienced gardeners place their herbs in brown bags to dry. A paper bag tied around the herbs will keep out humidity and dust. The extra protection is well worth it in the summer months and in coastal areas where humidity could spoil the herbs before they are completely dry. A paper bag is a must if you're harvesting seeds (dill or coriander) to catch the seeds as they fall from the drying stalks.

When the herbs are completely dried (one to two weeks), pull the leaves off the stems. Use a mortar and pestle to crumble broad leaves such as basil and parsley. Sunlight deteriorates flavor, so store the dried herbs in airtight containers in a cool, dark place.

BOUQUET GARNI

Bouquet garni is a centuries-old flavoring, a combination of parsley, bay leaf, and thyme. Traditionally used for soups, stews, and stock, bouquet garni simmers in the liquid long enough to flavor the broth, but it is removed before serving. When fresh herbs are available, several sprigs of parsley, one bay leaf, and a sprig of thyme are tied together with string so they can be easily removed. A miniature cheesecloth bag will keep dried herbs intact while their subtle flavors seep into the stock.

Bouquet garni from your own herb garden is an unusual and thoughtful gift and is sure to impress any good cook. Both the time and cost of putting them together is minimal. Bouquet garni can be packaged in several imaginative ways: individual cheesecloth bags, a jar of pre-mixed herbs with a wire tea ball, or a bouquet garni wreath, such as the one shown on the facing page.

The proportions are always the same—1 part thyme to 3 parts parsley and 1 bay leaf for each 4 quarts of stock. Each individual bag, premeasured for one soup pot, should contain 1 teaspoon thyme, 1 bay leaf, and 1 tablespoon (equal to 3 teaspoons) parsley. Some cooks also like to tie 6 peppercorns into each bouquet garni.

Cut cheesecloth squares 6" × 6". In the center of each square, mound the thyme, bay leaf, parsley, and peppercorns. Pull the corners of the square together to make a bag and tie it with white cotton string in a secure knot.

For a jar of bouquet garni, measure 1 part thyme to 3 parts parsley into a bowl and stir until the herbs are evenly mixed. Label the jar with instructions to add 1 bay leaf with each heaping tablespoonful of the herb mixture. The bay leaf will not distribute evenly in the jar, so it should be packaged separately.

An inexpensive wire tea ball (about $2.50) is a reusable substitute for individual cheesecloth bags. Consider giving one with a jar of pre-mixed bouquet garni. Porcelain and metal tea balls, which have holes, are not suitable because the crushed herbs will leak out.

Bouquet Garni Wreath

A bouquet garni wreath is a pleasing addition to your kitchen as well as to your cooking.

Materials
½ yard burlap
flat, plastic foam wreath form, 10″ in diameter
white household glue
¼ yard muslin
red thread
jute string
florist's wire
1 cup dried parsley
⅓ cup dried thyme
2 or 3 (¼-ounce) tins bay leaves

Equipment
scissors
books or other heavy weights
needle

Cut a circle, 16″ in diameter, from the burlap. Center the plastic foam circle on top of the burlap; then wrap the burlap around the foam circle, pulling tightly. On the inside edge of the wreath, pleat the extra fullness and tuck the loose ends under the edge, completely concealing the wreath form. Use a good bit of glue to secure the ends; then place the burlap wreath on waxed paper and weight it overnight.

Muslin bags, stitched in red like old snuff bags, hold the herb mixture. Cut two 6″ squares of muslin. Fold each piece in half and stitch across the bottom and along the side in a ½″ seam. On the top edge, press a ¼″ fold toward the wrong side of the fabric; then, concealing the raw edge, press under another ⅝″ fold. Stitch along the edge of the ⅝″ fold to make a channel for the drawstring. Pull the jute string through the channel with enough left over to tie around the top of the wreath. Make the second sack exactly as the first.

Stir the dried parsley and thyme until evenly mixed and fill each bag. Tie the filled muslin bags around the top of the burlap wreath. Add a bow of jute and a wire loop for hanging the wreath.

Select large, perfect bay leaves. (It may take several tins to get enough undamaged leaves for one wreath.) With just a drop of glue, secure the leaves on the burlap wreath. Begin to the left of the jute bow, layering the leaves so that they go in one direction and each leaf overlaps the glued end of the ones previously applied, as shown in the photograph.

Herb Bouquets

Love, good health, and long life are promises to the newlywed couple when the bride carries a bouquet of fresh herbs. Since ancient times, herbs have been important symbols in religious ritual and rites of passage, and even a modern bride can call on their legendary charms to bless her own wedding.

Marjoram in her bouquet recalls a Roman tradition of twining marjoram into crowns for a newlywed couple. All types of artemisia, such as southernwood and wormwood, were historically included in love potions. Lavender brings joy, and basil, love. And if that is not insurance enough, a sprig of lemon balm guarantees that all wishes will be fulfilled.

According to legend, herbs in the bouquet reveal much about the wedding couple. If the groom doesn't sneeze when sneezewort is in the bouquet, his love is not truly given. But he may feel justified in withholding his love if rue wilts in the bouquet, for that announces that his bride is not a virgin.

Herbs are not only more fragrant than most decorative flowers on the day of the wedding, but they are more easily preserved for anniversaries to come. Hanging in a dark, dry closet, the bouquet will dry by the time the bride returns from her honeymoon. If stored carefully, it will hold its shape for several years. Or the dried herbs can be crushed into a very special potpourri to freshen the new wife's lingerie.

The delicate scale of herb flowers and foliage suggests an old-fashioned Victorian nosegay. In the bouquets shown here, herbs were supplemented with decorative flowers, such as statice, baby's breath, and sweet william, which have the same dainty scale as herbs but add brightness to the subtle coloring of herb flowers.

A June bride marries too early to throw an herb bouquet; late July and August are the peak blooming times for herbs and thus the most colorful bouquets.

The bouquets shown on these two pages are a delicate mixture of many herbs and flowers, all of which are listed under the Materials. Select your favorites and arrange a bouquet of your own design.

Materials
Choose any of the following herbs and flowers:

Artemisia	Roman wormwood
Baby's breath	Rosemary
Broom	Sage blossom
Butterfly weed	Santolina (lavender
Chamomile	cotton)
Chives	Scented geranium

The flowers and herbs used in the bridal bouquet shown here include the following: baby's breath, chamomile (yellow and white), chives (pink), dead nettle (white or pink), lavender (pale purple), mint, rosemary, sage blossoms (deep purple), santolina, scented geraniums (lemon and old-fashioned rose), sweet william (mixed colors), and sweet woodruff.

Coreopsis
Dead nettle
Dwarf sage
Hyssop
Lamb's ear
Lavender blossoms
Lemon verbena
Mint
Oregano blossoms
Pinks
Purple basil (flowers
  and foliage)
Silver thyme
Soapwort
Sneezewort
Summer savory
Sweet william
Sweet woodruff
Tansy
Thyme (flowers and
  foliage)
Yarrow

oasis bouquet holder (includes a florist's sponge)
plastic bag
ribbon
lace

The day before the wedding, pick greens and flowers in the early morning. Let them stand all day in a cool, dark place, such as a garage, in a bucket of water. That evening they will be ready to combine in a bouquet.

Soak the plastic bouquet holder in water until the oasis—or florist's sponge—is saturated. Begin the bouquet by filling in a background of foliage. (Strip the lower leaves from the stems.) Make very small punctures in the florist's sponge. It is easier to change your mind if you haven't left large holes or broken areas in the sponge.

Add herb flowers and more greens, scattering them in small clusters of color. Add a layer of baby's breath last; it will visually tie together the different materials in the bouquet.

Note: A random scattering of color and varying materials throughout the bouquet creates an informal look. You can make a more formal bouquet with parallel borders of large leaves, such as tansy or scented geranium, working toward the center in concentric circles, reducing the size of leaves and blossoms as you near the center.

After completing the bouquet, sprinkle it lightly with water and put in a plastic bag in the vegetable crisper of your refrigerator. It will be ready for its part in the festivities at any time the following day.

Add ribbons and lace to the stem and the outside edge of the bouquet just before the ceremony.

The bouquets shown below were arranged with slightly different combinations of herbs and flowers. Left: baby's breath, butterfly weed (orange), dwarf sage, golden thyme, rosemary, sage blossom (deep purple), sneezewort, and yarrow (yellow). Right: baby's breath, butterfly weed (orange), Roman wormwood (gray and wispy), sage blossom (deep purple), santolina blossoms (yellow), silver thyme, skeleton rose geranium (large, green leaf), and sneezewort.

HerbVinegars

The over-the-counter drugs of nineteenth-century apothecary houses were herbal vinegars and teas, which were touted for their ability to cure a headache or to stop your hair from turning gray. If you're skeptical of the medicinal powers of herbs, consider that the taste of fresh herbs on a winter salad could indeed make you feel healthier.

Connoisseurs argue that the flavor of herbs preserved in vinegars is stronger and therefore preferable to dried herbs. Some herbs, such as tarragon, lose all flavor when dried and should only be preserved in vinegar. Mint vinegar on lamb and fruit salads also retains a freshness not found in dried mint.

Unusual flavorings are possible in a vinegar solution. The sharp, peppery flavor of nasturtium vinegar is sure to wake up winter taste buds.

Besides their distinctive flavors, herbal vinegars have another characteristic that separates them from commercial vinegars: beautiful, subtle colors. The color leaches from the herbs and herb flowers into the vinegar, and you'll want to collect cruets that show off the sparkling clarity of your homemade vinegars.

Materials
fresh herbs
vinegar (see recipes below)
large, clear jars with non-metallic lids
cheesecloth
clear decorative bottles or cruets

Equipment
funnel

Cut the herbs and reserve a few sprigs of each variety.

Loosely fill the large jars with fresh herbs, bruising the herbs slightly to release maximum flavor. (If you use dried herbs, measure ¼ to ½ cup for each quart of vinegar.) Cover the herbs with vinegar and seal the jars.

The steeping time varies depending on how you process the vinegars. If you do not warm the vinegar, it must steep for 1 to 2 months. You can speed the process up, however, with heat from the sun or from your range top.

Solar Vinegars: Put the large jars of fresh herbs and vinegar outside for 2 weeks. Taste for strength, and when the flavor is transferred to the vinegar, continue the steps below.

Range Top Method: Bring the vinegar almost to a boil before pouring it over the bruised herbs in the jars. Do not boil the vinegar as that can decay the herbs and ruin the flavor. When processed with warm vinegar, the herb vinegars will be ready for tasting in 6 to 10 days.

Remove the herbs from the jars and strain the vinegar through cheesecloth into decorative bottles. Add a fresh sprig of the appropriate herb to each bottle for decoration and identification.

SINGLE HERB VINEGARS
Tarragon: The gourmet's classic flavoring, tarragon vinegar is best when made with white wine vinegar.

Mint: Steep in cider vinegar for use in an English-style lamb sauce or on a fresh fruit salad.

Dill: Steep in cider vinegar and save for pickling brine.

Lavender blossoms: Lavender blossoms steeped in distilled white or white wine vinegar will give a pale lavender color. Versatile lavender vinegar adds tartness to a fruit salad and can be inhaled to cure a headache.

Chive blossoms: Process these blossoms in distilled white or white wine vinegar for a multipurpose vinegar with a delicate pink color.

Dark opal basil: These purple leaves will turn distilled white vinegar or white wine vinegar dark red.

Nasturtium: Use only a few nasturtium flowers in white vinegar because the color will leach quickly. The peppery flavor that adds such zest to summer salads can do the same to green winter salads or marinades.

COMBINATION VINEGARS
Eleven-herb vinegar: Use roughly equal amounts of fresh parsley, thyme, mint, burnet, basil, marjoram, lemon balm, rosemary, oregano, chives, and dill in white wine vinegar.

Garlic-tarragon: Put four peeled garlic buds, a handful of whole cloves, and loosely packed tarragon in a 1-gallon jug of cider vinegar.

Lemon: Lemon balm, lemon verbena, and a long, curled piece of lemon peel in distilled white vinegar makes a tart vinegar for fruit and green salads.

Herb Salt

Anyone who has cooked with fresh herbs or has savored their presence in a sauce or salad will go to any length to preserve the fresh herb flavor for year-round use. Herb salt is a very simple way to prolong the bounty of a summer garden.

Materials
fresh basil, parsley, thyme, and marjoram
celery leaves
fresh chives (optional)
kosher salt

Equipment
cake pan
salt grinder or food processor

Wash herbs and let dry on paper towels; then strip the leaves. Mix together the leaves of basil, parsley, thyme, marjoram, and celery so that the celery comprises about two-thirds of the mixed leaves.

If you wish an onion-like flavor in the salt, cut chives into 3" lengths and mix with the other leaves.

Cover the bottom of the cake pan with a layer of mixed herb and celery leaves. Pour a double layer of kosher salt over the leaves and repeat a layer of leaves and two layers of salt until the layers are about 1" deep.

With the oven set at 300°F., bake the herbs and salt for 20 to 30 minutes. When the herbs are "cornflake crisp," remove the pan and let the salt and herbs cool.

If you have a salt grinder, you can crumble the herbs slightly and put the mixture in the grinder as it is. For use in a salt shaker, put the herb/salt mixture in a food processor until it is finely ground.

PAPER: Handmade from Local Materials

In the early days of paper making in Japan, the individually handcrafted sheets of paper were rare and highly prized. When a letter was received, the reply was written on the same sheet of paper, fitted between the lines of the first message. Thus the addressee was literally forced to "read between the lines." This sixth-century recycling was a measure of the reverence for handmade paper—a reverence that has not diminished in Japan even now that handmade papers have become more plentiful.

True paper was invented in China, but the Japanese refined paper making and incorporated paper much more completely into their culture. (Although papyrus was used as a writing surface much earlier, it is not a true paper; true paper is defined by the way in which it is made.)

Twentieth-century America is now putting new value on paper. While disposable paper products were once a symbol of the affluence of America, the inevitable shortage that resulted has generated a new consciousness and has led to the recycling of even machine-made newsprint. As a parallel to this economic resourcefulness, craftsmen and artists all over America are beginning to make their own paper—both for correspondence and for artistic expression.

Watercolor artists have always valued handmade papers, most of which are imported from Japan. But other artists are beginning to use handmade paper as its own medium in flat collages where the paper is used like oil paint for broad areas of color and in sculptural wall hangings where layers of paper suggest mass.

SUITABLE PLANT MATERIALS

The first paper was made with local plants and household tools, and that has not changed. With plants from the garden and equipment from the kitchen, you can make your own beautifully textured paper. Iris, gladiola, begonia, and nasturtium are among the common plants whose fibrous leaves and stalks are ideal for paper. Beginning in late August—when many of these plants have stopped blooming—the materials are available for paper making.

The stalks and leaves from the following plants are recommended for use in paper making.

Iris
Begonias (all types except tuberous begonias)
Gladiola
Nasturtium
Cornhusks
Cattail stalks
Pampas grass stalks
Chicory
Yucca
Burdock

VARIATIONS IN TEXTURE AND DECORATION

Paper made entirely from freshly gathered materials will have a slightly rough texture. These papers are unsuitable for writing paper, but they are distinctive when used in decorative projects, such as the fans made of iris leaves which are shown on page 62.

The photograph below shows a sampler of papers made from common local plants. It takes a lot of plant material to make paper in this way—more than your yard may supply—but nurseries are often happy to let you trim their fading perennials.

If you want a smooth writing surface for stationery and Christmas cards, you can combine your own yard materials with prepared pulp, which can be ordered in dried sheets and processed with your local materials. (See Suppliers, page 150.) Although commercially prepared, the pulp is a natural material made from the fibrous leaves of the banana plant. One sheet of dried banana pulp costs from $3 to $4 and will make approximately 125 sheets of 6″ × 8″ note paper when combined with local materials.

An additional means of decorating your paper is to encase pressed flowers and leaves between two layers of wet paper. This is especially attractive in matched note paper and envelopes, as with the dried hydrangea shown in the photograph on page 61. Pressed leaves become a dramatic silhouette when encased, and petals of nasturtium and marigolds can add confetti-like color to paper.

Mould & Deckle

A mould and deckle is needed to scoop the plant fibers into thin sheets. A professional mould and deckle, which is exquisitely and tediously crafted of fine brass wires, costs from $200 for 8" × 12" stationery-size to $700 for easel-size sheets. Fortunately, you can make your own mould and deckle for about $2 with the following instructions.

Each different shape or size of handmade paper requires a separate mould and deckle: The mould and deckle dimensions shown here will make sheets 6" × 8", a good size for personal stationery or folded Christmas cards. (A diagram is also included for corresponding size envelopes, directions for which appear on page 61.) You need only to adjust the dimensions of the mould and deckle to make sheets of any size.

Materials
6' (¾"-square) pine molding
waterproof glue
8 brass screws (#4, 1" roundhead wood screws)
woven brass screening, 30 or 40 mesh (you may
    use aluminum or fiberglass window screening)
duct tape

Equipment
saw
ruler
screwdriver
staple gun with stainless-steel staples
scissors or wire cutters

From the pine molding, cut four 6" lengths and four 9½" lengths. Butt the corners of these pieces and line up two identical frames. (Diagram 1.)

Glue each corner of the frame with waterproof glue and reinforce with a brass screw. (Diagram 2.)

Stretch the screening tightly over *one* of the frames and staple it to the top of the frame.

Trim the screening so that it is flush with the outside edges of the frame. On the top of the frame, place the duct tape so that the edge of the tape is lined up with the inside edge of the frame, concealing the wood and staples. Wrap the excess duct tape around the sides and to the bottom of the frame. (Diagram 3.)

This screened frame is the mould. The second frame, the deckle, is used without screening.

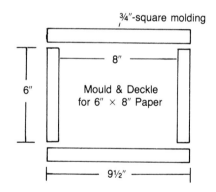

¾"-square molding

8"

6"

Mould & Deckle
for 6" × 8" Paper

9½"

Diagram 1

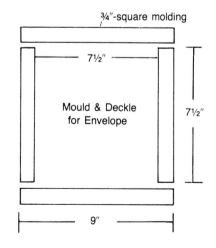

¾"-square molding

7½"

7½"

Mould & Deckle
for Envelope

9"

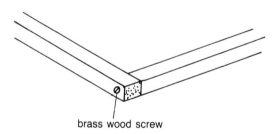

brass wood screw

Diagram 2

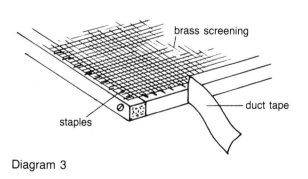

brass screening

duct tape

staples

Diagram 3

1

Preparing Plant Fiber

Materials
iris leaves or any of the other recommended plants suitable for paper making (page 57)
household lye crystals

Equipment
scissors or garden shears
stainless-steel or cast-iron pot with cover
measuring cup
rubber gloves
teaspoon measure
large stainless-steel spoon
colander
mallet or rolling pin

Wash the iris leaves and cut them into 1″ lengths.

Put the leaves into a stainless-steel pot and, with a measuring cup, add enough cold water to completely cover the plant material. Keep an accurate count of the amount of water added; then, wearing rubber gloves, add 1 teaspoon lye crystals per 1 quart water. Stir to dissolve and disperse the lye.

Caution: Even in this relatively weak solution, lye is highly caustic and can cause dangerous chemical burns. You must use a stainless-steel or cast-iron pot; you must wear rubber gloves; and you must add the lye to *cold* water.

Cover the pot and bring the solution to a boil. Lower the heat immediately to a simmer. Cook, stirring occasionally, until the plant material is soft and mushy. Cooking time for the iris leaves will be about 2 hours.

Wearing rubber gloves, drain the iris leaves through a colander and rinse several times. Repeated rinses will wash out the lye and remove much of the non-cellulose material from the plant fiber.

If you will be mixing local materials with prepared banana pulp, beating is not necessary. But for papers made completely from local materials, the plant fibers may need to be broken down further at this point. With a mallet or rolling pin, pound small amounts at a time until you see a change in the fibers (only a few minutes for each small clump).

Turning Plant Fiber into Paper

Materials
iris fibers, lye-processed and beaten
dried banana pulp in sheet form (optional)
small flower petals for color (optional)

Equipment
kitchen sink, plastic dishpan, or large ice chest (at least 12″ × 18″)
blender
mould and deckle
2 to 4 yards absorbent fabric (heavy denim, muslin sheeting, woolen felt, or a wool blanket with a low nap), cut into 16″ squares
sponge
2 boards ¾″ exterior plywood, minimum dimensions 16″ square
concrete blocks or other heavy weights
soft bristle brush
large glass or laminated surface (sliding glass door or kitchen counter)

Water is important to the bonding of the cellulose, and you work with a surprisingly small amount of fiber in a lot of water. Put 3″ to 4″ of water in the bottom of a deep container.

Scoop up about ¼ cup iris fiber and put it into a 1-quart blender. Fill the blender with water and process at a low speed for 1 or 2 minutes. Empty the blender jar into the deep container with the water. Continue mixing plant fiber and water in the blender in the above proportions until you have a thin, evenly distributed layer of fibers on top of the water in the large container.

For confetti-like coloring, add small, colorful flower petals, such as nasturtium and marigold, directly to the water and fiber mixture. Do not process the flower petals in the blender.

Note: If you are using dried banana pulp to supplement your own local materials, it should be combined in the blender stage. Cut from the sheet of dried pulp only as much as you think you will need (the entire sheet will make about 125 sheets of note paper). Cut the dried pulp into small pieces and soak it until it is thoroughly wet. When you put ¼ cup local materials (iris fiber) into the blender, add an equal amount of the well-soaked banana pulp before filling the blender with water.

Line up the deckle with the top, or screened side, of the mould, and wet them in clear water. Holding the mould and deckle firmly together (deckle should be on top), dip the two beneath the surface of the water and draw them out of the water with a layer of wet paper *covering the entire surface of the screen*, as shown in photograph 1. If there are holes or thin

2

3

4

5

spots in the layer, you do not have enough plant fiber. Process more fiber with less water in the blender and add to the mixture.

You must now transfer this wet sheet of new paper to another surface so you can use the mould again; the transfer process is known as "couching." Wet the squares of absorbent fabric and wring out the water so that the paper will cling to the fabric.

Lift the deckle off the mould and turn the mould over—with the paper side down—onto a square of damp fabric, as shown in photograph 2. On the back of the mould, press repeatedly with a sponge to release the paper. Gently lift the mould, leaving the paper on the fabric, as shown in photograph 3. If you occasionally tear a sheet when lifting the mould, pull the paper from the fabric and put back into the blender to reprocess.

Note: If the paper does not consistently stick together at this point, the cellulose has not bonded. If you are faced with this situation, you must try one of two remedies: go back and beat the fibers more thoroughly or add dried banana pulp to help the bonding. In the latter remedy, you can substitute recycled envelopes or white writing paper for the banana pulp. They should be treated the same way—cut into small pieces and soak thoroughly; then blend with water to a creamy consistency and add to the pulp and the water mixture in the sink.

If the new paper adheres consistently to the absorbent fabric, put another damp fabric square on top of the first sheet of paper as shown in photograph 4. Repeat the dipping and couching procedures, building up a stack of fabric and papers.

Put several layers of paper and fabric (up to a dozen) between two plywood boards and weight the boards to press excess water out of the paper. Professional craftsmen use a book binding press, but you can substitute bar weights, concrete blocks or your own body weight with the boards on the floor, deck, or patio. Work where the water will not damage anything as it is pressed out.

After pressing, remove the top fabric cover and gently pull one sheet of paper off the fabric. (The wet paper is very fragile at this point; if it tears, put it back into the blender.) Using a very soft bristle brush, smooth the paper onto a glass or laminated surface to dry, as shown in photograph 5. A picture window, sliding glass door, or laminated counter is a convenient surface. (If you get really involved with paper making and have the storage space, you can cover a large plywood board with laminate as a drying board.)

Allow the paper to dry thoroughly. This may take from 3 to 24 hours to dry, depending on the weather, but it can be speeded up with the use of a fan.

Encasing Pressed Flowers & Leaves

Materials
dried banana pulp or recycled paper
local plant materials, lye-processed and beaten
small flowers and leaves, dried and pressed

Equipment
same as those for Turning Plant Fiber into Paper

For a smooth writing surface, use twice as much dried banana pulp (or recycled paper) as local plant fiber. Soak the dried pulp, cut into small pieces, and put ¼ cup in a 1-quart blender.

Prepare the local fiber as explained in Turning Plant Fiber into Paper (page 59). Add about ⅛ cup prepared fiber to the banana pulp in the blender.

Fill the blender with water, process at a low speed, and pour the mixture into the large container. Repeat until you have a thin, even layer of fiber on top of the water in the container.

Dip the mould and deckle and transfer one sheet of paper to the absorbent fabric. Place the pressed materials on top of this first sheet.

Dip another sheet of paper and carefully line it up directly on top of the first sheet. The wet sheets will fuse together, trapping the pressed flowers and leaves between the layers. If you use moss or grasses which extend beyond the edge of the paper, let the paper dry and then trim away the excess.

Envelopes

Encasing dried materials is an excellent way to make matching note paper and envelopes. Diagram 1 on page 58 shows the dimensions for a mould and deckle to make envelopes that will fit 6″ × 8″ note-paper. Follow Diagram 1 below for directions on folding your handmade paper into envelopes. Seal the handmade paper envelopes with hot wax.

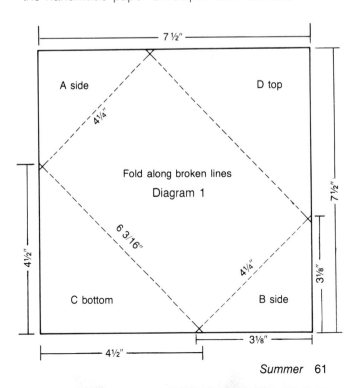

Fans

Materials
local plant materials, lye-processed and beaten
dried banana pulp in sheet form (optional)
cattail stalks (you may substitute pampas grass)
pampas grass, raffia, or vine

Equipment
same as those for Turning Plant Fiber into Paper
round mould and deckle or embroidery hoop over
    square mould (refer to instructions on page 58)
masking tape

The paper fans are a variation of the method described in Encasing Pressed Flowers and Leaves (page 61).

The fans are made by encasing cattail or pampas grass between two round layers of paper. The paper layers can be made completely from local material; the bottom fan in the photograph was made from iris leaves. Prepared banana pulp was used for the all-white fan at the top of the photograph, and the blue-on-white fan pictured in the middle is banana pulp colored with a textile dye.

Note: For the round mould and deckle used in making the paper fans, you can cut two wooden rings of the same size from plywood. Finish the mould with screening and duct tape as instructed for the stationery-size mould on page 58. Or, a round wooden embroidery hoop may be substituted for the deckle and used in combination with a larger, square mould.

Prepare the local plant fibers or banana pulp as described in Turning Plant Fiber into Paper (page 59). The fans work better with a thicker pulp, so use less water in the blender process.

Dip the round mould and deckle into the pulp and transfer the paper to the absorbent fabric just as you would a sheet of note paper, sponging the back of the mould to release the paper.

If you are using the large wooden embroidery hoop as a substitute for the deckle as described above, remove the pulp around the outside of the hoop before transferring the paper to the absorbent fabric.

Align five long cattail stalks over the paper circle so that the thick ends of the stalks come together in a point outside the area of the paper. This will serve as the handle. Loosely tape these stalks together.

Dip the mould and deckle again and transfer the second piece of paper to the fabric, carefully aligning it with the first paper to encase the stalks.

If you want to add a second color to the fan, as shown with the blue-on-white fan in the photograph, place the open deckle frame over the top layers of paper and use a turkey baster (cut the end off so that the opening is ½″ in diameter) to control the addition of the second color of pulp. You can also pour the second color for broad areas of color. Lift the deckle away and cover the new fan with damp fabric.

As with note paper, a number of fans can be pressed at one time.

Very carefully lift the fan and stalks and brush onto a glass or laminated surface. Leave the tape on the ends of the cattail to help support the stalks until the fans are dry. Once dry, the fan is surprisingly sturdy.

Wrap the stalks with pampas grass, raffia, or vine to form a handle.

AutumnCrafts

CORNHUSKS: Nature's Wrapping

Whether for use in dolls or harvest wreaths, cornhusks require very little special preparation. You can allow cornhusks to dry right on the stalk, and because outside husks shield them from dust, they need little cleaning. For those readers who do not have access to a cornfield, packages of cornhusks can be ordered through the mail. (See Suppliers, page 150.) A convenient alternative is to save and dry the husks from the corn you purchase at the grocery store.

Some craftspeople prefer to press the husks flat between the pages of heavy books so that they will retain a flat shape when dry. Use waxed paper on each side of the husks to protect the pages, and weight the books for at least 2 weeks.

The dry husks are quite brittle and will tear easily. Therefore, you must soak the husks in order to manipulate them in craft projects. Soak the dried cornhusks in hot water for 10 minutes and cover them with a damp cloth or towel to keep them moist and pliable. As you work, remove only a few cornhusks at a time from the towel.

Since cornhusks will tear easily along the ribs, always cut the husks so that the longest dimension runs in the same direction as the ribs.

Make sure your cornhusks are completely dry before storing them in an airtight container. Should the cornhusks become damp and mildew, soak them in a solution of ¼ cup chlorine bleach to 1 gallon water for several hours. Spread the cornhusks on newspaper to dry completely; then seal in an airtight container.

DYEING CORNHUSKS

If you wish to add color to your craft project, cornhusks can be dyed with packaged fabric dyes.

The cornhusk flowers shown on pages 65-67 were dyed in this manner. Choose soft colors that occur naturally in the fall landscape; strong colors are not appropriate to the cornhusks.

Mix 1 teaspoon fabric dye with 1 quart steaming-hot tap water. Pour this dye bath into a wide, shallow casserole. Add more dye bath if needed to a depth of ½". Immerse the flat cornhusks so that they do not touch each other and leave for 5 minutes. Remove the husks from the dye bath to test the color shade and repeat the process if you wish a darker color.

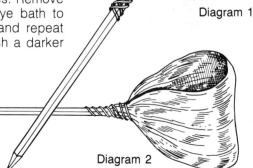

Diagram 1

Diagram 2

Cornhusk Wreath with Osage Oranges

Osage oranges, often called hedge apples, horse apples, or bowwood (because the Indians carved their bows from the tough wood of the tree), are a striking textural addition to the soft gold coloring of cornhusks. Additional accents are squirrel "cobs"—pine cones that have been chewed by squirrels, leaving a reddish "cob."

Materials
cornhusks
2 or 3 green osage oranges (hedge apples)
florist's wire, 16-gauge
florist's picks
straw wreath form, 16" in diameter
2 dozen pine cone squirrel "cobs"

Equipment
oversized books or magazines
waxed paper (optional)
books or other heavy weights
knife
aluminum foil
cookie sheet

Place cornhusks between the pages of an oversized book or magazine and weight the top with books for 10 days or until the husks are dry and pressed flat. (Use waxed paper between the husks and the pages to protect the pages from stain.)

Slicing crosswise as you would slice a tomato, cut the osage orange into ¼"-thick sections. Cut the florist's wire into 4"-long pieces and push one length of wire through the center of each section of osage orange.

Lay the osage orange slices on a foil-covered cookie sheet and heat in a 200° F. oven for 4 hours. Remove osage orange slices from the oven and set aside to cool. When the slices have cooled, pull the ends of the wire together and secure to a short florist's pick in a lollipop shape. (Diagram 1.)

Wrap wire around the top of the wreath form and make a loop for hanging.

Soak the cornhusks for 10 minutes to make them pliable and less brittle. Fold each cornhusk in half. Gather the ends together and twist a wire pick tightly around the bunched end. (Diagram 2.)

Cover the straw wreath form with the folded cornhusks, starting at the bottom of the wreath and working to the right so that all cornhusks lie in the same direction and overlap each other slightly.

Space the osage orange slices around the wreath, nestling each one between the cornhusks.

Fasten squirrel "cobs" to florist's picks and scatter around the wreath for added interest.

Cornhusk Flowers

Materials
cornhusks
fabric dye
22-gauge florist's wire
florist's tape
masking tape (optional)
dried berries and pods (optional)
white household glue

Equipment
pencil
lightweight cardboard
scissors

Soak the cornhusks in hot water for 10 minutes and work with them damp. If you wish to add subtle color to your bouquet, you can dye husks with packaged

fabric dyes as explained in the section on Dyeing Cornhusks, page 64.

On lightweight cardboard, draw a pattern for each different petal shape. A few petal patterns are shown below to get you started, but you can make your own pattern to imitate any flower. An important rule to remember when cutting petals from cornhusks is to make the base of the petal fairly wide in order to attach the petal to the wire stem.

Lay the patterns on the cornhusks so that the ribs of the husks always run from the center of the flower to the tip of the petal, never *across* a petal shape. Use the same pattern in multiples of 5 to 8 cut from the same color. The more petals you use, the fuller the flower. Draw around the pattern on the cornhusks with a pencil and cut along the marks.

With florist's tape, wrap the first petal around one end of a florist's wire stem. Tape consecutive petals on the outside of the first, shaping each petal with your fingers. On a broad, flat flower, glue a black-eyed Susan or dried berries in the center to conceal the wire.

Continue wrapping the wire stem with florist's tape. If the green tape is too conspicuous in a tan and brown arrangement, you can cover the green stem later with masking tape.

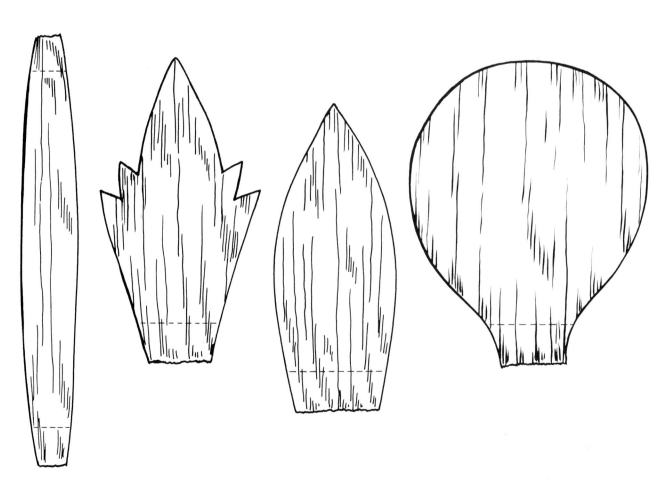

Cornhusk Pioneer Women

Materials
cornhusks
florist's wire
beige thread
cotton ball
corn silk or embroidery thread
white household glue
small dry twigs

Equipment
scissors
ruler
pencil
felt-tip pen

Soak the cornhusks for 10 minutes in hot water until they are pliable. Spread the cornhusks on a soft towel to keep them damp while you are working with them.

Arms

Cut a piece of wire 7½" long. From the cornhusks, cut a rectangle 1½" × 9". Place the wire on the long edge of the rectangle and roll the husk tightly around the wire. At each end, the husks will extend ¾" beyond the wire; fold the ¾" extra cornhusk back to form a loop and tie with sewing thread. (Diagram 1.) Tie the center of the tube.

For the sleeves, cut two pieces of husk, each 2" × 5". Wrap one piece loosely around one "wrist," overlapping the wrist by ½" but with most of the husk extending beyond the arm. (Diagram 2.) Wrap and tie tightly at the wrist, gathering the fullness into the tie. Fold the sleeve back toward the center, creating a puffed sleeve at the wrist, and tie the opposite end of the sleeve tightly around the center between the arms. (Diagram 2.)

Repeat at the other wrist to make a second sleeve.

Head and Chest

Cornhusks have a ribbed side and a shiny side. In wrapping the head, make sure the shiny side is out so that the ink face drawn on later will not be distorted by the ink following the ribs.

Roll a small bit of cotton into a tight ball, about 1" in diameter. Cut a piece of cornhusk 4" × 6". With the husk skiny side down, place the cotton ball halfway along one long edge. Holding the cotton ball in place on the edge closest to you, roll the husk lengthwise away from you, enclosing the cotton head in a tube.

With a firm grip on the head, twist one side of the husk as close as possible to the head. Fold the twisted husks back behind the head and tie all husks together just below the head to make a neck. (Diagram 3.) The twist at the top of the head will be covered later by hair.

Just below the neck, separate the front and back husks of uneven lengths and slide the arms between them, centered beneath the head. Wrap thread in a cross pattern, front and back, to secure the arms. (Diagram 4.)

Dress

Cut two strips of cornhusk, each 5" × 9". Place one piece in front and one in the back so that they overlap 2" below the neck with most of the husk extending above the head. At the neck, wrap string around these husks and tie. (Diagram 5.) Then fold the husks down as the underskirt.

Cut several long strips of husk ¾" wide. Wrap these, one at a time, over one shoulder with the end below the waist on the opposite side. (Diagram 6.) Alternate with a second piece over the opposite shoulder. Gather the husks at the waist and tie as tightly as possible.

Cut an apron 2" × 5". Position it in the front so that it overlaps the waist for only 1" and extends above the waist, covering the head. Tie it in place with a single thread. (Diagram 7.)

Raise the arms of the doll above her head. Place four to six large husks around the waist on all sides; the husks should just overlap the waist and extend over the head of the doll. Wrap and tie these husks in place at the waist. (Diagram 8.) Fold them down as a skirt along with the apron, and trim the husks evenly along the bottom.

Hair and Kerchief

Glue a little bit of corn silk or embroidery thread across the top of the head as hair. Cut a piece of cornhusk 2" × 4". Wrap the piece over the top of the head, just behind the hair line, and around to the back and glue it in place. (Diagram 9.) Tuck the loose edges in toward the head in a kerchief style and glue where they overlap.

Wait two days before drawing the eyes with a felt-tip pen to make certain there is no moisture left in the husks, which would make the ink run.

Bundle of Sticks

Break thin, dry twigs into 3" lengths. With florist's wire, tie the sticks into a bundle of about 25. Conceal the wires with thin strips of husk.

Cut two long strips of husk, each 1" wide. Wrap one from the top of the bundle over the right shoulder and under the left arm, beneath the bundle, and tie. Wrap the other strip around the bundle, over the left shoulder, under the right arm, and tie in back.

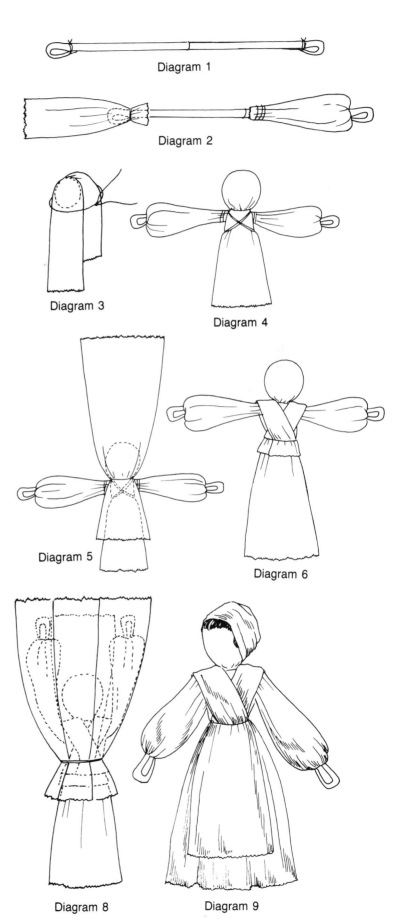

Diagram 1

Diagram 2

Diagram 3

Diagram 4

Diagram 5

Diagram 6

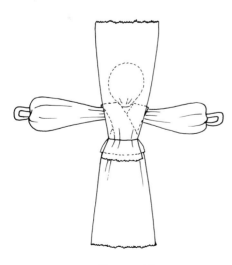

Diagram 7

Diagram 8

Diagram 9

Cornhusk Angel Mobile

Materials
cornhusks
florist's wire
cotton balls
beige thread
white household glue
corn silk or embroidery thread
clear filament (fishing line)
clear nail polish

Equipment
scissors
ruler
pencil
straight pins
small bottles or other weights
hair clip
felt-tip pen
bowl
needle-nose pliers

Soak the cornhusks in hot water for 10 minutes or until they are pliable. Spread the cornhusks on a soft towel to keep them damp while you are working with them.

Arms

Cut a piece of florist's wire 4″ long. From the cornhusks, cut a rectangle 1½″ × 4½″. Place the wire on the long edge of the rectangle and roll the husk tightly around the wire. (Diagram 1.) With sewing thread, tie the center and both ends. At each "wrist," tie a very narrow strip of husk over the ties to hide the thread. (Diagram 1.)

Make sleeves from a strip 1″ × 4″. Fold this piece lengthwise over the arm. Gather the sleeve at the center and tie. (Diagram 2.) Pull the sleeves down at the open wrist ends and pin the arm and sleeves onto a flat board to hold that shape until the husks dry overnight.

Head

Cornhusks have a ribbed side and a shiny side. In wrapping the head, make sure the shiny side is out so that the ink face drawn on later will not be distorted. (On the ribbed side, the ink would tend to follow the ribs.)

Roll a small bit of cotton into a tight ball about the size of your thumbnail. Cut a piece of cornhusk 4″ × 6″ for the face and gown of the angel. With the husk shiny side down, place the cotton at the midpoint of one long edge. (Diagram 3.) Holding the cotton ball in place on the edge closest to you, roll the husk lengthwise away from you, tightly enclosing the cotton head in a tube.

With a firm grip on the head, twist one side of the husks as close as possible to the head. (Diagram 4.) Fold the twisted husks back behind the head and tie all husks together just below the head to make a neck. (Diagram 5.)

Just below the neck, separate the front and back husks and slide the arms between them, centering the arms beneath the head. Wrapping thread in a criss-cross pattern, front and back, secure the arms within the gown. (Diagram 6.)

Robe

To make a robe to conceal the wrappings, cut two strips of cornhusk, each 1¼″ × 3½″. Place one piece in front and one in the back so that the wrappings are just covered by one end and the lengths of the husks extend above the head and shoulders. (Diagram 7.) Wrap and tie these husks in place with a firm knot at the neck. Then fold the husks down over the body as a robe.

If you want your angels to "fly" on a mobile or on your Christmas tree, shape them while the cornhusks are still damp. Prop the angel so that she faces a vertical surface, such as a wall or a box, with her skirt extended over a flat surface. Put a small bottle on top of her skirt and a book beneath the very end of her

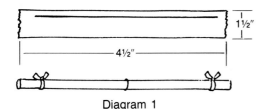

Diagram 1

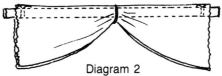

Diagram 2

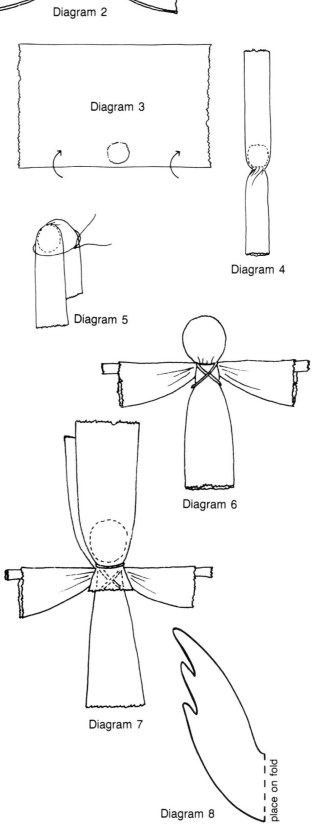

skirt so she will dry overnight into a graceful "in-flight" curve, as shown by the angels in the photograph.

Wings and Features

Fold a 2½" square of cornhusk in half; then, using the pattern in Diagram 8, draw and cut out a pair of wings. Glue these on the back of the angel and hold in place with a flat hair clip until the glue dries.

For hair, you can glue cornsilk onto the head for a fluffy, halo effect, or you can use embroidery thread for a smoother hairdo. With the embroidery thread, wrap the thread about 25 times around a 2" square of cardboard. Tie all the threads together at one edge of the cardboard; then cut through the threads at the opposite edge. The tie where the threads are gathered will make a part; glue it to the top center of the head. Tie the hair together again at the back of the neck, if desired.

Wait at least 2 days before you draw the eyes to be sure there is no moisture in the husks, which would cause the ink to run.

Mobile

To make the mobile, cut a piece of florist's wire 4" long and another piece 5½" long. With needle-nose pliers, make a small loop in each end of the wires and give the wires a slight curve by shaping them around a bowl.

Tie 8"- to 10"-long pieces of fishing line around the neck of each angel. Tie an angel to each end of the shorter wire and adjust the fishing line so that the angels hang at different lengths. Tie another piece of fishing line to the center of the wire and slide it along the wire until you find the balance point where the wire hangs horizontally. Fasten the line in that spot with a drop of clear nail polish.

Pull the opposite end of this line through one end of the longer wire and adjust the line so that it is 5" long before knotting it.

Tie a third angel onto the other end of the long wire; adjust the length of the line there so that she will not hit the other angels as the mobile rotates.

Tie a piece of fishing line to the center of the long, top wire and slide the line along the wire until you find the balance point. Secure the line at the balance point with a drop of clear nail polish. Hang the mobile to check the balance and unobstructed rotation; then put a drop of glue on all the knots to keep them from shifting.

Corncob Pipes

Many people swear corncob pipes provide a better, more natural smoke than any other kind of pipe. And because they are not expected to last forever, the bowls are often replaced, which further insures a fresh tobacco taste.

Materials
corncob
cane

Equipment
pocket knife
electric drill
heavy-gauge wire

Dry the corncob and the cane outside for a week before making the pipe.

Cut a crosspiece about 2" long from the dry cob. With a knife, hollow the cob for the pipe bowl, leaving a base and sides at least ⅜" inch thick.

About ¾" above the base, drill or scrape a hole in the side of the pipe bowl; the hole should be slightly smaller than the diameter of the cane stem for a snug fit.

Cut the cane into a piece 6" long for the stem, and use a straight piece of heavy wire to clear a passage through the cane. Wedge the cane stem into the pipe bowl.

Cornstalk Indian & Canoe

Materials
cornstalk (cut while it is still green)
thread

Equipment
pocket knife

From an undamaged part of the green cornstalk, cut a piece that includes a joint at each end. Cut a section out of one side of the stalk and remove the soft center pulp of this section just as if you were digging out a log canoe. Make the first cuts so that you can remove the pulp in one piece for use as a pontoon. (Diagram 1.) If the section of pulp is longer than 3", cut into a 3" length.

Make two small slits, one in each side of the hollow canoe, positioning the slits so that they will support a horizontal pontoon. From the tough outside bark of a scrap piece of cornstalk, shave a thin straight bar ⅛" × 4" to 6". Slide one end of this bar through the slits and push the opposite end into the soft pontoon float. (Diagram 2.)

From the scrap piece of stalk, carve a feather, bow and arrows, and an oar out of the harder, outside bark. Notch the ends of the bow and tie thread, tautly stretched, to each end.

The soft interior of a length of cornstalk is easy to carve into an Indian figure. Before carving, mark the placement for the eyes, shoulders, and hands. (Diagram 3.) Then shape with shallow cuts. Cut another piece of soft pulp about 2" long and just wider than the hollow of the canoe. Wedge the Indian in place at one end of the canoe; then push the extra piece of pulp into the hollow to hold the Indian tightly in place.

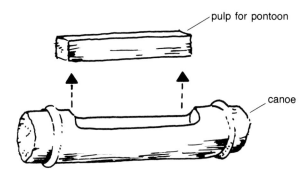

pulp for pontoon

canoe

Diagram 1

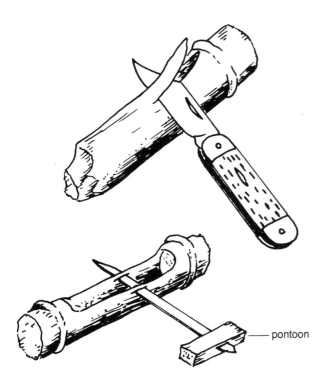

pontoon

Diagram 2

Diagram 3

VINES: Nature's Rope

Honeysuckle, grapevine, and kudzu—those vines you ignore on the roadside and curse in the garden—are extraordinarily beautiful when used in a craft that emphasizes their graceful forms. Wrapped into full, tight wreaths, these vines have a charm and naïveté reminiscent of folk art. There are practical advantages to making vine wreaths: not only are the materials widely available and free, but they are also often found growing in a spot where they should be cut back.

A wreath is the symbol of hospitality, so why wait until the Christmas season to display this traditional form of welcome? One vine wreath can serve as a versatile base for year-round use, particularly if it is freshly decorated to greet the change of season. The sturdy vine base, which takes only minutes to make, will last for many years.

GATHERING VINES

Vines can be cut for wreaths all year long, but September through April is the best time to harvest them. Strike out into the woods with a pair of sharp hand shears and a ball of string. Cut grapevines, kudzu, and honeysuckle near the roots and tug until you free a long runner. Clip the leaves and branches off as you pull the vines from bushes and trees, and it will be easier to pull the runners free. Leave a few of the spiraling fingers on the grapevines for intriguing forms in your wreath. (See special instructions below for cutting bittersweet and wisteria vines.)

Stretch the runners out lengthwise in small bundles. Then wind a bundle of runners around your forearm, from hand to elbow, and tie them into circles for transporting. If you plan to strip the bark from honeysuckle, tie it into circles small enough to fit into a soup pot because it must be boiled for several hours. This technique is explained in the section on honeysuckle.

MAKING THE WREATH

Start with a long, thick vine. Hold the thicker end of the vine in one hand and loop the vine as you would a garden hose into a circle about the size you want the finished wreath to be. On the next loop, pull the full length of the vine through the inside of the circle. As if you are wrapping ribbon around the wreath in candy cane stripes, wrap the vine to the outside of the circle and pull it back through the inside of the circle in long spirals. (Diagram 1.)

Some vines are fairly stiff, so you will be able to pull through the circle only about two times in each loop. However, the smaller, more flexible vines can be pulled through with the wraps much closer together, which will result in an obvious spiral pattern in the finished wreath. By wrapping the vines in and out in this way, the wreath will hold its shape without rope ties. Tuck ends of each vine securely inside the wreath.

GRAPEVINES

It is easier to make a grapevine

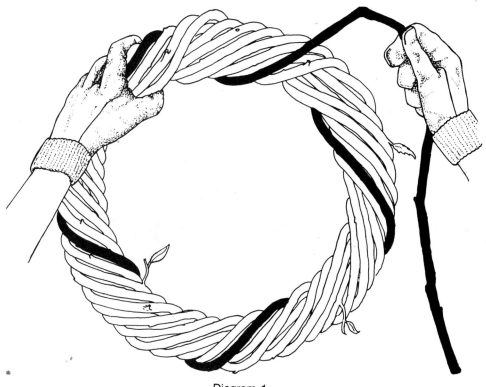

Diagram 1

wreath on the spot than to carry the vines home. Because of their thickness, grapevines cannot be used for small wreaths, but they make a generous wreath, suitable for a 30"-wide door. You might also consider hanging a grapevine wreath over a fireplace mantel or dining room buffet.

The interesting spiral tendrils on grapevines are especially effective in a wreath.

KUDZU

Kudzu vines, about ¼" in diameter, are thinner than grapevines and are well-suited for smaller wreaths. (Of course, the smaller the vine, the more required to make one wreath.)

Right: A basic kudzu wreath with a bright kudzu blossom for color is shown hanging in front of the lush greenery of kudzu vines—plenty for many more wreaths!

Below: This grapevine wreath is dressed with bittersweet (left) and with apples (right) for two distinctive—and equally striking—decorations.

BITTERSWEET

In demand for its yellow and orange berries, wild bittersweet is also one of the most flexible vines to work with and should not be discarded when you collect the berries in the fall.

Bittersweet can be wrapped into small, 8″ wreaths as well as wreaths up to 2′ in diameter. Bittersweet makes an excellent, tight base on which to glue pine cones, and it is substantial enough to support the weight of fruit without distorting the wreath shape.

The most pliable vines are those between ¼″ and ⅜″ in diameter that branch off the thicker primary vine. Cut these at the joint with the larger vine. You must strip the vine of berries and branches to make the wreath, but the small branches with berries will dry easily and can later be wedged within the wreath base, as they are in the grapevine wreath shown in the photograph on page 75. Branches at least 3′ long can be wound into the wreath.

WISTERIA

Although it has a better reputation than most other vines, wisteria benefits from judicious pruning, and, like the less desirable vines, wisteria will quickly replenish itself if cut correctly. Do not disturb the thick trunk vine; cut only the secondary runners and leave at least four buds on the runner on the plant, counting from the trunk vine.

HONEYSUCKLE

The warm reddish color and rough texture of honeysuckle bark make a rustic wreath. The wrapping technique is the same as that described above. However, when the bark is stripped away from the vine as it was in the honeysuckle wreath pictured here, dressed for the four seasons, the effect is very delicate and refined.

Tie the vines into small tight circles as you pull them free. The bundles must be small enough to fit inside your largest soup pot.

Cover the vines with water and boil for 3 hours. After boiling, untie the bundles and strip the bark from the vines by pulling each runner through a towel gripped tightly between your fingers.

Because it is so thin, it takes a lot of honeysuckle to make a wreath, and you probably do not have enough large pots or enough range burners to boil all the honeysuckle at once. After you have stripped the bark from one batch, tie the runners together and store them in a cool place until you have enough for a full wreath. Soak the dried honeysuckle in water for about 30 minutes to make it flexible again before attempting to shape the vines into a wreath.

Fine honeysuckle runners need to be wrapped around a basket to maintain a wreath shape until they dry. A half-bushel basket was the base for the wreath pictured on these two pages. Wrap each runner around the basket, tucking the end back into the wreath. Once the honeysuckle dries, it will hold its shape, so there is no need for the in-and-out wrapping used with larger vines.

To retain the pale blond color of a stripped honeysuckle wreath, hang it outside for only short periods of time. After a few weeks in damp or rainy weather, the vines will mildew and discolor. To remove light mildew, soak the wreath in the bathtub in a mild solution of water and chlorine bleach.

The stripped honeysuckle wreath shown on these two pages is accented for the four seasons: fresh azalea blossoms in the spring, seashells in summer, a plaid bow for autumn, and red and green ribbon and magnolia leaves for winter.

Quarter-Moon Wreath

This pine cone and bittersweet vine wreath is unusual in its simple quarter-moon shape. The wreath is also distinctive because of imaginative collecting—including a spruce aphid gall, which is, in fact, a diseased part of the tree but which adds an interesting natural form to the wreath.

Many combinations of cones, nuts, and seedpods can be attractive. The wreath shown here used the following natural shapes against a bittersweet vine wreath:

rhododendron
sweet gum balls
spruce aphid gall
white pine cones
Japanese red pine cones
pecans, filberts, English walnuts, almonds, and
    Brazil nuts
scotch pine cones
European beech nut cones
Douglas fir cones
Carolina hemlock cones
eastern hemlock cones

Materials
bittersweet vines
cones, nuts, and seedpods
white household glue or electric glue gun with
    glue sticks

Equipment
garden shears

Strip bittersweet vines of berries and branches and twist into a wreath form (Diagram 1, page 74).

Arrange the larger cones on the wreath first and then fill in with the smaller cones, pods, and nuts. When you are satisfied with the arrangement, glue each piece in place on the vine wreath.

Vine-Wrapped Vases

These attractive, rustic vases are particularly suited to hold wildflower bouquets. They are actually nothing more than jars wrapped with honeysuckle vines, and they can easily be completed in less than an hour! Any shape jar or bottle may be wrapped with vines. (The large vases shown in the photograph contained instant iced tea.) Wine bottles with slim necks would make perfect vine-covered bud vases.

The interesting nubbly texture shown on the vases in the photograph was made by prominently exposing the ends of each vine. For a smoother effect, simply make sure the vine ends are butted together and glued securely to the jar.

Materials
jar or bottle with label removed
honeysuckle or any other smooth, flexible vine

Equipment
electric glue gun with glue sticks or epoxy glue in a
    syringe
pruning shears or razor knife

Apply a bead of glue about one-quarter of the way around the midsection of the jar. Press one end of the vine into the glue and hold firmly until the glue sets (or dries). As soon as the glue is dry, begin wrapping the vine around the jar. Wrap tightly and evenly, positioning each new wrap as close as possible to the previous one.

When you have about 4″ of vine left, apply another bead of glue alongside the last wrap. Pull the vine tight, holding the end, and continue to hold until the glue dries. Cut off the loose end with a razor knife or pruning shears. Continue wrapping with another length of vine.

Once you have wrapped the top half of the jar in this manner, wrap the bottom half, going in the same direction on the jar. As you work, keep pushing the vines tightly together toward the middle of the jar. No part of the jar should show between the vines once you have finished wrapping.

Use your own imagination in finishing your vases. Add one or several layers of the same vine in a narrow band around the top and bottom to give the vase more dimension. Or use a larger diameter vine (either stripped or natural). For further variety, you can wrap this band in a criss-cross manner rather than in regular rows.

Apply a bead of glue around the entire lip of the vase to hold the last row firmly in place. Do the same on the bottom. Allow to dry for 1 to 2 hours and you're ready for a bouquet.

Nature Weavings

Leaves, grains, seedpods, and berries—the distinctive shapes and colors of autumn—can be preserved and showcased in nature weavings. The simplicity of the weavings and the lacy weblike structures allow nature to speak for itself.

By the time autumn comes, many plant materials from the woods and fencerows are beginning to dry naturally, but because they can be destroyed by rainy weather, preserving them for use indoors requires careful timing. Cut plants that have airborne seeds, such as pampas grass, cattails, and milkweed seedpods, before they go to seed or they will shed in the house. Hair spray—the cheapest brand you can buy—will help to prevent flying seeds.

Berries add appealing color to any nature weaving, but, unfortunately, the species which dry well are limited. Nandina and sumac clusters, if cut at their peak, can be easily dried by hanging the clusters upside down for a few weeks. (Sumac berries will darken as they dry.) Bittersweet will also keep its color inside the house, but it will shed more easily once inside. Cut rose hips as soon as they turn and dry them upside down.

The seed stalk of the poke berry is another popular addition to nature weavings because of its luscious purple color. Remove the berries, which are poisonous and will permanently stain fabrics, and then dry the purplish stalk in silica gel.

Some seed heads, such as crepe myrtle, black-eyed Susans, and rhododendrons, do not require any special drying processes and are excellent materials to add contrasting forms to your nature weavings. For specific instructions on drying methods, refer to the section on Dried Flowers, page 38.

Autumn Colors
in a Weaving

Materials
vegetable oil
natural materials (given in the order in which they appear in the weaving photographed)
    mountain maple leaves
    maple seed clusters
    pearly everlasting
    dogwood leaves
    teasel
    dead oak branches with goatsbeard lichen
    brake ferns
    ash flowers
2 fairly straight sticks, each 18″ to 20″ long and ⅝″ to ¾″ in diameter
100% wool yarn in beige for warp (may substitute cotton or linen)
100% wool yarn in earthen colors for weft
clear filament (fishing line)

Equipment
newspaper
2 nails
hammer
dowel, 24″ long and ⅝″ to ¾″ in diameter
twine or jute
scissors
pruning shears
long, curved upholstery needle

GATHERING AND DRYING MATERIALS

Dip leaves and ferns in vegetable oil soon after collecting; then layer them between sheets of newspaper and leave flat for several days. Repeat the procedure so that the leaves and ferns absorb more oil. The vegetable oil preserves the color of the natural materials and helps them retain a fresh look.

Air dry flowers, seeds, and teasel by hanging them upside down in a dark, dry spot until rigid (1 or 2 weeks).

SETTING UP THE WEAVING FRAME

Hammer two nails about 20″ apart into the top frame of a doorway. From these nails, hang the dowel with twine loops, trapeze-like, at a height conveniently above eye level. Make sure the dowel is level; it will be the temporary hanger while the weaving is being constructed. (Diagram 1.)

Cut two pieces of twine or jute, each 11″ long, and knot each piece into a 5″-long loop. Hang these loops from the dowel, *inside* the existing loops, and slip one stick into these loops. (Diagram 1.)

Cut two pieces of twine, each 10′ long, and knot each piece into a 59″-long loop. Hang these loops from the dowel, *between* the original loops and the 5″-long loops. Slide a second stick into these loops. (Diagram 1.) Adjust the loops near the ends of the sticks to represent the shape and size of the finished weaving. Hang rocks or shoes as weights at the bottom to keep the framework—and thus the warp—straight.

TYING THE WARP

Use a continuous strand of wool yarn from a ball or spool to wind the warp. Tie the warp thread to the right end of the dowel just inside the three loops. Drop the ball of warp yarn *in front of the frame* and pass it front-to-back under the bottom stick; then pull the yarn toward you over the top of the stick and to the right of the warp yarn. (Diagram 2.)

Hold the ball of warp in the left hand and with the right hand, pull a long, loose loop of yarn from the ball toward you and to the right of the first warp yarn. Still holding the loop, bring the ball of yarn back over the top of the stick, around the back and under, and then, on the front side, up through the underside of the loop in your right hand. (Diagram 3.) Pull the yarn tightly to the back of the frame to complete the first knot and warp thread.

Pull the ball of yarn firmly to the top of the frame

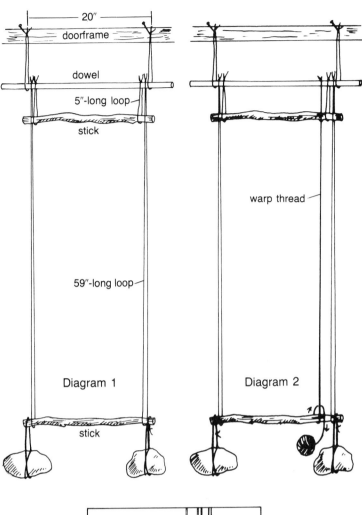

Diagram 1

Diagram 2

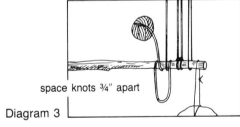

Diagram 3

space knots ¾″ apart

from the back and over the top of the *dowel*, from back to front. Repeat the process of bringing the warp down the front, knotting it around the bottom stick as described above, and passing it over the dowel at the top from back to front. Space the warp knots about ¾″ apart, working toward the left until the warping is completed. Cut the warp yarn and tie the end near the short loop at the left end of the dowel.

Remove the 59″-long loops of twine at this point to make weaving easier. To do this, remove one weight at a time, very carefully; then slip the long loop off the stick and replace the weight. Repeat on the other side of the frame. Note that the top stick is suspended within the top of the frame. This stick is independent so that it can be easily lifted out of the way when work space becomes cramped in the final stages of weaving.

WEAVING

Measure and cut a length of yarn for the weft that is equal to five times the width of the bottom stick plus a few inches. Tie one end of the yarn onto the warp thread on the right side. Thread the other end of the yarn into a long, curved, upholstery needle.

Weave the needle in and out, closing the warp above the bottom stick. (Diagram 4.) Pass the needle behind the back warp and in front of the forward warp threads across the entire width of the frame from right to left. Adjust the tension of the yarn so that it is firm, but not so tight that it distorts the warp threads.

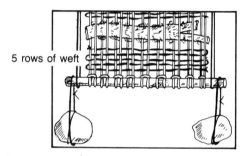

5 rows of weft

Diagram 4

It is now easy to pass the needle back through from left to right because the warp threads are separated in an alternating pattern. On the next run from right to left, again weave behind the back warp and in front of the front warp to pull them together. Weave across the width of the panel two more times for a total of five weft threads. Tie a simple knot onto the far left warp thread and cut off the excess yarn.

With one hand, spread the warp with alternate threads in opposite directions and place a green lichen-covered branch within the space cleared with your hand. Press the branch firmly toward the weft threads. (Diagram 4.) With pruning shears, cut away any part of the branch that extends outside the weaving frame.

Select a yarn to match or harmonize with the material and cut a measured length as before, five times the width plus a few extra inches. Tie the yarn end onto the far right warp thread and proceed to needle-weave the weft for five rows. Keep the warps evenly spaced and the outer edges of the weaving as vertical as possible; if the outer edges pull toward the center, the weft yarn is being pulled too tightly. After the fifth weft, knot the yarn onto the left warp thread.

Continue to add to the weaving, working from the bottom up and contrasting adjacent materials. Save small, easy-to-weave materials for last because the warp becomes very short and tight near the top. End with a band of weft threads close to the top stick. (Diagram 5.)

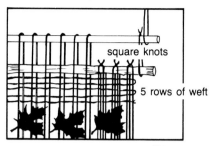

square knots

5 rows of weft

Diagram 5

FINISHING

Keep the 5"-long loops firmly in place at the top of the weaving; they will support the hanging while the warp threads are being tied. Beginning at the right side, cut the first two warp threads at the dowel and tie them together in a square knot on the top of the upper stick. (Diagram 5.) Trim the excess beyond the knot to ¼". Continue cutting and tying warps, working across to the left until all the warp threads are removed from the dowel. Remove the weights from the bottom stick and the dowel from the top.

Tie a long thread or fishing line to each end of the top stick for hanging.

Landscape Weaving

Materials
large metal hoop
multi-ply, medium-weight yarn for wrapping hoop
multi-ply, fine yarn for warp
dried grasses such as wheat, rye, broom corn, oats, or broom sedge
clear glue
assorted textures and colors of yarn for weft (landscape)

Equipment
crochet hook
tapestry or yarn needles sized for the yarns chosen
scissors

The first step is to cover the metal hoop with a medium-weight, multi-ply wool yarn. You can do this in several ways: cover the frame with lark's head knots (reverse double half hitches) (Diagram 1), blanket stitches (Diagram 2), or a single crochet stitch (Diagram 3).

Diagram 1

Diagram 2

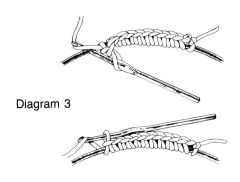

Diagram 3

WARPING THE LOOM

"Warp" refers to the supporting vertical threads stretched within the metal hoop. Use a fine, tightly twisted yarn in a neutral color for the warp. If the warp is the same color as your wall, it will "disappear," leaving the woven landscape to "float" on the wall.

At the left side of the hoop, slightly above the horizontal center, slide the crochet hook on the back through one strand of the yarn that covers the metal hoop. Loop the warp yarn around the hook and pull the loop to the inside of the hoop. Enlarge this loop enough to pass the ball of warp yarn through it; pass the ball *over the front of the hoop* and through the loop. Holding on to the loose end of yarn on the outside of the hoop, pull the inside piece to tighten the loop. This fastens the warp yarn to the hoop. This is the only place you will pass the yarn *over* the front of the hoop to secure. All other warps are fastened only to the ridge of yarn in the following manner: Working from the back of the hoop, loop the yarn around the hook (Diagram 4) and pull the loop to the inside. Enlarge the loop and pass the ball through it from back to front. (Diagram 5.)

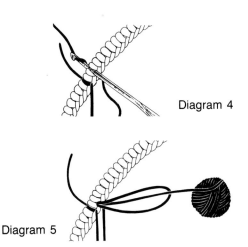

Diagram 4

Diagram 5

Repeat this procedure across the width of the hoop to secure the warp yarn to the ridge of yarn covering the metal hoop. All warp yarns should be ¼" apart. Keep an even tension on the warp threads, but do not pull them so tautly that they will distort the hoop. When all warp threads are in place, adjust the tension if necessary. Then knot the ends of the warp to maintain the even tension.

WEAVING WITH GRASSES

With the hoop on a flat surface, position the grasses in a pleasing composition. For a good design balance, avoid placing grasses in the exact center of the circle. Gently weave the grasses in and out of the warp yarns to hold them securely in place. You may need to use a tiny drop of clear drying glue on the warp yarn to hold a seed head upright.

WEAVING THE LANDSCAPE

The foreground, mountain line, and clouds in the weaving shown here not only introduce a three-dimensional depth to the weaving, but they help to firmly hold the vertical grasses in place. With a tapestry or yarn needle, weave the foreground in a light color, encasing the ends of the grasses in the close weave. When you reach the end of one piece of yarn, pull the loose end to the back of the weaving. Knot it on the back side to a second piece of yarn and continue weaving.

Since dark colors recede, the mountain line should be woven in a darker colored yarn than the foreground so that it will appear to be farther away. Consider using mohair or a similar fuzzy yarn for the clouds for a light, airy texture.

Shallot Ropes

Shallots are the gourmet's choice within the onion family. With proper curing and storing, they will last through the winter months and until the next year's harvest. Good ventilation is critical, however, in making the shallots last, so a braided rope is not only an attractive, but also a practical way to store them with maximum air circulation. Onions can also be braided for storage, but they will not last as long as the shallots.

When the first shallot stalks begin to turn yellow and collapse in the fall, knock over the entire row, but leave the bulbs in the ground for 2 more weeks. After that time, pull the bulbs and lay them out in a single layer, preferably on screening that will provide maximum air circulation. Let them dry for 1 week in a cool, dry spot with good ventilation.

Tie the stalks of three shallots together with string and start a braid as though you were braiding hair. After 2″, add one shallot to the center strand; cross the shallot once more in the braiding pattern and continue adding one shallot to the center strand. When you add a shallot to the center strand, treat the two stalks as one while you continue braiding. Although the shallot stalks are short and will run out often, you may reach a point where you are treating three stalks as one in braiding. Continue adding one shallot to the center strand until the rope is as long as you like. (Diagram 1.)

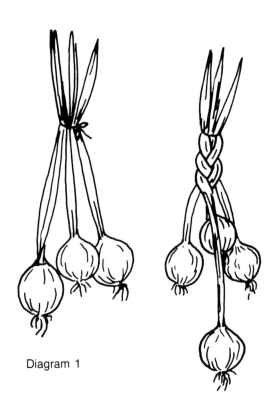

Diagram 1

Black Locust Weed Pot

A weed pot is so named because it is perfect for holding a sprig of berries or wild grasses—without water—until they dry. Folk wisdom has it that the later the locust is cut in the fall, as the sap is slowing, the better your chances are that the bark will adhere. The finished height of your pot should be equal to the diameter, but allow 2″ more in the log for trimming. Whenever possible, include lichen in the cut section and take care not to damage the lichen in working with the log.

Materials
freshly cut black locust log, 4″ to 6″ in diameter
wood preservative
satin finish polyurethane varnish

Equipment
saw
hand brace and ¾″ bit or electric drill and flat spade
  bit
wood lathe and turning tools
sandpaper
chisel
small paintbrush
soft rag

The black locust log must be dried quickly after cutting to prevent large cracks. If the log has already begun to crack, saw ½″ to 1″ off each end to remove the cracks before baking. Bake the log in a 225° F. oven, turning it once, for 12 hours, or longer if the log is more than 6″ in diameter. Quick-drying in the oven will create many small cracks, which are better than one large crack which would result from air drying.

Drill a hole ¼″ deep in the center of the log. Work slowly because the cracks may cause the bit to wander off course. Center the log on a wood lathe and shape the top with a narrow deep gouge or scraping chisels. Work slowly while cutting the bark to prevent chipping.

Trim the bark on the base of the pot just slightly. Cut the bottom in a concave form, leaving a level rim on the outside edge so that the pot will sit level. (Or, you can sand the base flat with a belt sander.)

Sand the cut sections of the wood on the lathe. If you do not have a lathe, carefully sand the edge between the bark and the wood by hand. Remove the pot from the lathe, chisel the excess from the bottom, and finish drilling the hole in the top about 3″ or 4″ deep.

A small amount of wood preservative between the bark and the wood will prevent fungus growth in a humid climate. Brush polyurethane on the cut wood without letting it drip onto the bark. Immediately wipe it off with a soft rag and let dry. Repeat several times.

Rosemary & Yarrow Wreath

Materials
florist's picks
straw wreath form
rosemary
rabbit tobacco
yarrow
goldenrod
cones of white spruce
Siberian iris seedpods
button stems
cinnamon sticks
fixative (hairspray)
large bow
whole cloves
nylon netting

Wire small clusters of rosemary onto florist's picks and push the picks into the straw wreath form along the inside and outside edges. Wire the rabbit tobacco to florist's picks in bunches and fill in fully between the borders of rosemary.

On the face of the wreath, add yellow yarrow all around, interspersed with goldenrod.

Cut a few cones to resemble roses (see Pine Cone Roses, page 133). Attach the "roses" to florist's picks and space the cones around the wreath to balance the arrangement.

On the bottom of wreath, arrange the white spruce cones, Siberian iris seedpods, button stems, and cinnamon sticks that have been attached to florist's picks.

Spray the entire wreath with a fixative, such as hair spray, and add a suitable bow.

Wrap the whole cloves in squares of nylon netting, secure to florist's picks, and fasten to the wreath under the bow.

Dried Herb Wreaths

The two dried wreaths shown above are strikingly dissimilar because of the materials used, but the technique used to create the two is the same. Both wreaths started with a background of silver king artemesia. The wreath on the left is filled in with reddish brown astilbe flowers and yellow tansy flowers with an accent cluster of brown teasel. The more delicate wreath on the right was accented with silvery lunaria (money plant), purple oregano flowers, tiny strawflowers, and baby's breath.

For your wreath, choose from among the general materials listed below, or create your own design with whatever is available from your garden.

Materials

straw wreath form	statice
artemesia	oregano flowers
astilbe flowers	teasel
yarrow	lunaria (money plant)
tansy flowers	U-shaped florist's pins
straw flowers	florist's wire

Most straw wreath forms are sold wrapped in green plastic. The green background is suitable to full, thick wreaths of Christmas greenery, but wreaths of dried materials are usually more delicate and "airy" in appearance and look best if the dried materials are set against the beige color of the straw. To remove the plastic, simply cut through one layer and unwrap the plastic from the wreath.

Air dry the herbs and flowers as described on pages 38 and 50. Then cut the dried herbs into small sprigs, no longer than 5".

Twist a hanging loop of florist's wire around the straw wreath form before adding the herbs.

Attach the material you have selected as the background to the wreath first. Cluster several short sprigs and secure them to the straw form with a U-shaped pin. Work in one direction from the starting point all the way around the wreath so that all materials will point in the same direction.

Scatter secondary materials evenly throughout the wreath, using U-shaped pins as needed.

Pumpkin Totem Pole

Legend has it that early settlers carved angry faces on pumpkins and set them in their windows at night to deceive and hopefully to frighten away any marauding Indians. As times grew safer and the settlers became more relaxed, they continued carving the pumpkin faces as a harvest ritual—a tradition we still follow today.

While it is no problem getting children interested in trick-or-treat, many parents worry that little constructive experience comes from Halloween. You can turn pumpkin carving into an intriguing learning experience, however, if you involve the young ones in researching historic carved faces.

Totem poles are a uniquely American art form, and the library is a source for photographs and drawings of those carved by Indians of the Northwest. Of the totem poles that have been documented, most were carved by the Kwakiutl, Tlingit, and Haida tribes.

Look beyond just the facial pattern on totem poles for other ideas to adapt to pumpkins. For instance, a totem pole was traditionally topped by a smaller head. They were also embellished with stylized eagle wings, beaks, and horns. You can make beaks or wings from the discarded pieces of pumpkin you cut from eyes and mouths. Since these pumpkins are stacked, you will not need to replace the tops, which can be fashioned into realistic or fantastic appendages.

Materials
7 pumpkins
metal fence post
florist's picks
votive candles
long matches

Equipment
short, sharp knife
large spoon or scoop
pencil

Carving hasn't changed since the days of the pioneers. Simply cut the top out of each pumpkin and discard the seeds. Draw a face on the pumpkin in pencil and then cut along the lines with a short, sharp knife.

Stabilize the pumpkin totem pole on a metal fence post. Drive the pole into the ground up to the cross bar and then slide the pumpkins, one at a time, down the post. It is best to stack the pumpkins in order of size, with the largest on the bottom. (You may have to puncture the bottom of the pumpkin first.) As you add each pumpkin, trim the top so that the next pumpkin will sit level.

With florist's picks, attach any desired appendages as mentioned above. Put several votive candles in each pumpkin as you go—it is not easy to lift the top and add candles later. You will need long matches to light the candles.

Don't leave all this fun for the children; consider a pumpkin carving party and competition for the adults, too. The early settlers may have been successful in frightening people away with carved pumpkins, but with a pumpkin totem pole in your yard in the twentieth century, you're going to *attract* a lot of attention.

Tulip Tree Masks

The leaves of the tulip poplar—the great big, bright yellow ones that fall in October—have a distinct, catlike shape. Wicked eyes torn in the leaf can quickly turn it into a pre-Halloween mask that is both inexpensive and, for a few weeks, replenishable.

Nature's Picture Frames

Like so many aspects of our lives that have grown more casual, family portraits are now more likely to be made in the woods than in a formal studio setting. Many photographers specialize in candid shots of children at play in the trees, on the beach, or in the sandbox. It can be difficult, however, to find a suitably informal frame for such relaxed poses.

Take a cue from the photograph and go back outdoors to find twigs, bark, leaves, berries, or moss to cover your own frame. For instance, if you photograph a child climbing a tree, cover the frame with dried, pressed leaves from the tree. Twigs and bark on a frame will help express an "all boy" personality captured in a photograph. Or you can simply repeat a color in the photograph with a color from nature—yellow gingko leaves or golden maple wings, and red sumac berries (avoid white sumac which is in the family of poison oak and similarly irritating). White birch bark can be a striking frame for a slightly dark photograph that has white highlights.

The only limitation on the type of covering you choose is that the natural material must adhere to the flat surface of the frame. Leaves can be pressed flat by weighting them between layers of waxed paper in a heavy book. Maple wings will lie flat in an intriguing shingle effect if you cut the stem and seed off. Flexible bark, such as both white and silver birch, can be split and weighted to lie flat. Thicker bark and twigs adhere to frames if glued on in small pieces. Berries that remain firm after they dry, such as sumac, can be held onto the frame with a thick layer of glue.

Not only will you enjoy an original frame, custom made for the photograph, but you will save money by making your own flat, unfinished frames. With a purchase of glass and table easels, most do-it-yourself framing houses will let you use their tools.

These frames were made from inexpensive pine lath, available at a lumberyard. The soft pine lath can be easily cut with a hand saw and a small miter box. (A box about 12" long costs $3 to $5.) Dimensions are given in the chart for several standard-size frames.

Materials
soft pine lath (see chart for dimensions)
white household glue
screen molding (see chart for dimensions)
cardboard table easel
bark, twigs, berries, or leaves

Equipment
miter box
hand saw
ruler
staple gun with 5/16"
   staples
paper
scissors
metal edge
matte knife
framing stapler
waxed paper
heavy weights

Alternate the angle of the saw in the miter box so that each piece of lath you cut is a boat shape. (Diagram 1.) All measurements should be made on the longer side of the boat shape, as shown.

In addition to the four boat-shaped pieces that will make the frame itself, you must also cut four pieces of screen molding. (Dimensions are given to the right of the frame size in the chart.) These narrower pieces will be glued to the back of the frame to form a lip to secure the glass, photograph, and table easel.

With white household glue, glue four frame pieces together along the mitered corners to form a frame. (Diagram 2.) When the corners are dry, align the four narrower pieces of screen molding on the back of the frame. The measurements given in the chart allow approximately ¼″ lip on the inside to hold the glass and table easel. Glue the back pieces to the frame and to each other along the mitered corners. (Diagram 3.)

Allow the glue to dry and reinforce the corners with 5/16″ staples from the back. If the natural material you're planning to use is dark or will not completely conceal the light-colored frame, stain the frame to match the color of the cover material.

Once natural materials are glued on, you should avoid unnecessary handling. For this reason, it is best to put the photograph, glass, and table easel in place before glueing the natural materials to the frame.

You will not be using standard glass sizes, so ahead of time, cut a paper pattern equal to the size of the glass needed (the inside dimensions of the back supporting frame). Give the pattern to the framing shop to cut your glass.

Use the same paper pattern to cut cardboard table easels. Pick a standard-size easel that is closest to your pattern size. Place the pattern on top of the table easel so that the hinged stand will be slightly above and to the left of the center of the paper pattern. (Diagram 4.) This placement provides the most stability. With a metal ruler and a sharp matte knife, cut the easel to fit the pattern.

With the frame upside down, place the glass in, the photograph face down, and cover with the table easel. With the framing stapler (borrow it from your do-it-yourself framing house), secure all layers. With glass, table easels, and a fee for using the framing shop, these frames cost from $3 to $6 each.

Before glueing on the natural materials, trim your paper pattern slightly and lay it over the glass to protect it from glue. Spread a thick layer of white household glue on the frame and arrange the materials. Trim the seeds off maple wings, but let them extend beyond the frame in uneven lengths until they dry. Do the same with gingko and other leaves. After the glue is dry, cut along the edges of the frame in a straight line with sharp scissors.

Bark is hard to cut on the frame, so arrange it in an appealing pattern and cut it to shape before glueing. Both leaves and bark should be covered with waxed paper and weighted overnight. The first time you pick up a frame covered with berries, a few may drop off, but they are surprisingly permanent after that.

Photo Size	Pine Lath	Screen Molding
3½″ × 3½″	24″ of ⅞″ lath cut 4, each 5¼″	24″ of ⅝″ screening cut 4, each 5¼″
3½″ × 3½″	24″ of 1⅛″ lath cut 4, each 5½″	24″ of ⅝″ screening cut 4, each 5½″
3½″ × 5″ (shown in diagrams)	24″ of ⅞″ lath cut 2, each 6″ cut 2, each 5¼″	24″ of ⅝″ screening cut 2, each 6″ cut 2, each 5¼″
4″ × 6″	30″ of 1⅜″ lath cut 2, each 6½″ cut 2, each 8″	26″ of ⅝″ screening cut 2, each 5⅞″ cut 2, each 7¼″
5″ × 7″	36″ of 1⅜″ lath cut 2, each 9⅜″ cut 2, each 7¾″	30″ of ⅝″ screening cut 2, each 8½″ cut 2, each 6½″
5″ × 7″	36″ of 1⅝″ lath cut 2, each 9⅝″ cut 2, each 7⅝″	30″ of ⅝″ screening cut 2, each 8½″ cut 2, each 6¼″
6½″ × 6½″	36″ of 1⅝″ lath cut 4, each 9″	36″ of ⅞″ lath cut 4, each 8¼″

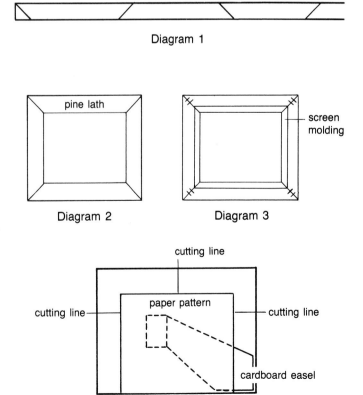

Diagram 1

Diagram 2 — pine lath

Diagram 3 — screen molding

Diagram 4

cutting line

paper pattern

cutting line

cutting line

cardboard easel

STRAW: A Golden Bounty

Primitive farmers believed that the forces that controlled the cycles of birth, death, and rebirth—exemplified in the planting and harvesting of crops—were temperamental and should be treated carefully so that they would continue to bless the harvest. Thus the custom arose, apparently independently in countries as far apart as ancient Egypt and Finland, of treating the last shock of corn (the universal term for any grain) as a special talisman. The last stalk was woven into what was called a "dolly" and, depending on where the ceremony was taking place, was either brought inside to be broken up and used in the spring for planting or was tossed up for the scythes of the harvesters.

Because the "dollies" are so pretty, they are fascinating to craftspeople today. The intricate woven designs are continually being deciphered and duplicated. The tiny tokens make wonderful Christmas ornaments, package decorations, wall hangings, and party favors.

The straw itself is a material of great beauty. The plaiting of corn dollies allows the full stalk plus the seed head to be used. However, the stalk of the straw can be used for marquetry work with very pleasing results. In marquetry, the entire stalk of the grain is split open and flattened. These pieces of straw are then glued and cut to form designs in much the same way as thin strips of wood veneer are used in wood marquetry.

The grains used for straw crafts are primarily wheat, oats, and barley. (The "corn" of the talisman corn dolly was wheat or oats.) The grain used for craft work must be hand-harvested; machine gathering crushes the stalks and seed heads. Even though our projects call for traditional grains, why not experiment with other straw that may grow naturally in your area? The preparation will be the same, no matter which straw you use.

If local straws are not available, you can order different types of straw through the mail. (See Suppliers, page 150.)

TOOLS AND EQUIPMENT

Craft knife: Used to cut out designs for work in marquetry.

Hole punch: Used to cut precise circles in marquetry.

Scissors: Used to cut straw above the joints on the stalk. (Work with an old pair of scissors because straw will dull the blades.)

Wallpaper trough or large pan: Container in which to soak straw.

Old towel: Used to wrap straw in after it has been soaked.

Seam ripper: Used to split straw.

Iron: Used to flatten and remove all the moisture from tempered split straw.

Carpet thread or heavy thread: Used to tie straw together for plaiting or weaving.

Sandpaper: Used to roughen shiny outside surface of straw so that all pigments and finishes will bond to it.

White household glue: Applied with a brush full strength to the inside flattened surface of the straw. Adds durability when cutting out designs and seals straw before and after coloring or finishing.

Tracing paper: Used in making design patterns for cutting and as a base for glueing straw ribbons for marquetry.

Masking tape: Used in marquetry to hold down tracings and straw ribbon to be woven.

Dowel or pencil: Used as a core to plait around.

Raffia or Swiss straw: Used in some projects for wrapping around straw or other forms, such as metal rings, used with straw work.

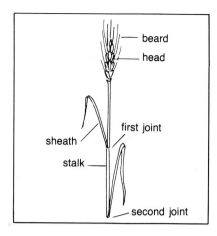

TERMS

Head: Top portion of straw where the grains form.

Beard: Long, fine fibers that grow out of the grains in the head of wheat and most other types of straw.

Joints: Notches dividing the segments on the straw stalk.

Sheath: The leaf that grows up and out of either the second joint or the bottom of the straw stalk.

Tempering: Returning the moisture to the straw by soaking it. This process is necessary to make the straw pliable for plaiting or splitting.

Plaiting: Braiding or weaving the straw in round or flat forms.

Splitting: Cutting open the tempered straw for marquetry.

Straw ribbon: Straw that has been split and ironed flat.

Straw ribbon sheet: Straw ribbon glued to tracing paper for marquetry.

Marquetry: Arranging split straw, or ribbons, on a surface to form various patterns and shades.

TYPES OF STRAW

Wheat: Gold in color, has beard, preferred for plaiting.

Beardless Wheat: Gold in color, has no beard, preferred for plaiting.

Black-Bearded Wheat: Gold in color, with a black beard, preferred for plaiting.

Brown Wheat: Brown in color, has beard, preferred for plaiting.

Oats: Cream to gold in color. Head consists of 15 to 20 kernels

Wheat · Beardless Wheat · Black-Bearded Wheat · Brown Wheat · Oats · Barley

which hang separately. Suggested for use in marquetry and plaiting.

Barley: Cream in color, short head, long beard. Suggested for use in marquetry and plaiting.

PREPARING THE STRAW

Cutting

For straw that is to be used in marquetry, cut straight across the straw 1″ below the head, just above and below the first joint and above the second joint on the straw.

For straw to be used in plaiting, cut straight across the straw just above the first joint. Cut straw at a slant 1″ below the head. The slant is necessary for joining the straw together for added length. Straw below the first joint is considered waste and is not used for plaiting.

Note: Some types of weaving or plaiting designs require leaving the head on the straw.

Soaking

It is best to soak only the amount of straw that can be worked in 2 hours. Place straw in a trough, bathtub, or large pan for soaking. Fill the container with cold or lukewarm water. Allow the straw to soak 20 to 30 minutes if it is to be used for plaiting or weaving. For marquetry, soak the straw 30 minutes to 1 hour (longer soaking time is sometimes required when using second joints for marquetry), or until the straw feels soft enough to be split or worked.

Bend the straw. If it does not crack, it is ready to be worked with. If left in the water too long, the straw will become dark in color, bruises or spots will show, and the heads will swell. Sometimes this discoloration is desirable for straw marquetry.

After removing the straw from the water, roll it in an old towel. Leave the straw wrapped in the towel for at least 15 minutes. Keep the straw rolled in the towel while you work to prevent it from drying out. Any unused damp straw must be spread out to dry so that sprouting and/or mildew will not occur. Straw may be resoaked as needed, but it will become darker in color with each soaking.

MARQUETRY

Preparing the Straw Ribbon

With a seam ripper, split one side of the straw by running the ripper from one end to the other. (Diagram 1.)

Set your iron on a dry heat synthetic setting and prepare a work surface with a soft cloth for ironing. Carefully unfold the straw at one end and iron down the inside (rough) surface. (Diagram 2.) Hold down the open end of the straw with a finger while ironing to the other end. This will prevent straw from sliding around.

Turn the straw over to its outside (shiny) surface and press flat with the iron. To make sure that all the moisture is removed from the

straw, you may need to iron each piece more than once. Should a crack or split occur, continue ironing out every drop of moisture; most splits will fuse back together. If your design calls for darker shades of straw, set the iron on a high, or cotton, setting.

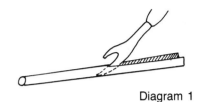

Diagram 1

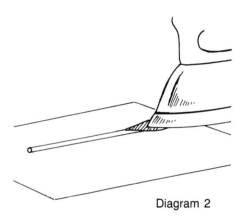

Diagram 2

Working with Straw Ribbons

To make a straw ribbon sheet, coat a piece of tracing paper with white glue. Glue prepared straw ribbons, rough side down, onto the tracing paper. (Diagram 3.) Protect the outside surface of the straw ribbons with a soft cloth. Weight this sheet with a book until the glue dries.

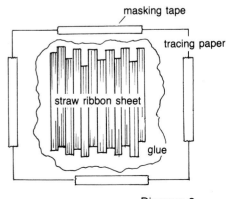

masking tape

tracing paper

straw ribbon sheet

glue

Diagram 3

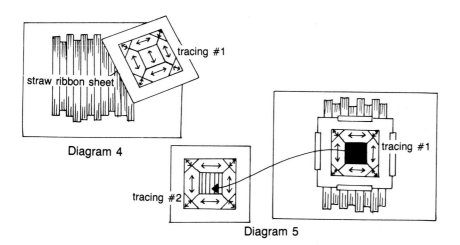

Diagram 4

Diagram 5

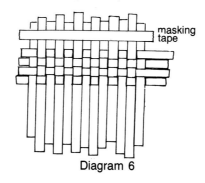

Diagram 6

Coloring and Finishing the Straw Ribbon

Most pigments and other finishes will not adhere well to a slick, shiny surface. For this reason, straw ribbons should be sanded on the outside (shiny) surface before applying one of the following finishes. Be sure to work in a well-ventilated room when using any type of paint or stain.

Paste food coloring: Add a small amount of paste food coloring to a little boiling water. Mix well. Soak the straw in this solution until practically all of the water has evaporated. This method tints the straw, giving it a soft, subtle color. When straw ribbons have dried, apply glue to the inside (rough) surface.

Acrylic paint: Brush glue to the inside (rough) surface of the straw ribbon; let dry. Sand the outside surface. Apply acrylic paints to the sanded, outside surface of the straw with a paintbrush. It will dry quickly, leaving an opaque appearance. Mistakes may be gently scraped away after the paint has dried.

Glass stain: Brush glue on the inside (rough) surface of the straw; let dry. Sand the outside surface. Apply glass stains to the sanded surface of the straw with a heavily loaded paintbrush in a flowing motion. The stain will dry quickly. Generally, the light to medium colors are transparent enough when dry for the natural straw to show through.

Water-base wood stain: This procedure can be used on the entire surface of an object that is covered in natural straw marquetry. Brush glue on the inside (rough) surface of the straw; let dry. Sand the shiny side of the straw; then apply a coat of spray acrylic finish to that surface. Allow the finish to dry. Using a paintbrush, apply the wood stain; then wipe off excess with a soft cloth or tissue. The stain dries quickly. Coat the straw with a second coat of spray acrylic finish.

Water-base wood stains enhance the grain of the straw, but if you apply the stain directly to the

With a pencil, draw the patterns for your straw marquetry design on two sheets of tracing paper. Label the pattern tracings No. 1 and No. 2. Draw arrows on each sheet to indicate the direction the straw should run. (Diagram 4.)

Note: The angles at which the straw ribbons are placed in your design will create subtle shades with the overall marquetry design.

Protect your work surface with a heavy sheet of cardboard. Place the straw ribbon sheet on top of the cardboard, straw side up.

Lay tracing No. 1 on top of the straw sheet and secure it in place with masking tape. With a craft knife, cut out each section of the design, rotating the tracing according to the direction of the arrows after each section is cut.

Glue the straw pieces as they are cut from tracing No. 1 onto tracing No. 2. (Diagram 5.) Protect the straw ribbons with a soft cloth. Weight down tracing No. 2 until the glue dries.

Using a craft knife, cut around the outside edge of tracing No. 2. Glue this straw design to the desired surface—such as a wooden box—and allow to dry. Trim any overhang with a craft knife.

Complete by applying one of the finishes described in Coloring and Finishing the Straw Ribbon.

Woven Straw Work

In woven straw work, you should always work with straw ribbons slightly longer than the dimensions of the design pattern. Lay natural or pigmented ribbons in vertical rows, side by side. Using masking tape, attach the top ends of the straw ribbons to a work surface.

Working in a horizontal direction, run a straw ribbon over and under the vertical ribbons. Alternate the weaving in the next row. Continue this process to the bottom of the vertical straw ribbons. (Diagram 6.)

Remove the masking tape. Glue the woven straw ribbons to a sheet of tracing paper; then protect the straw with a soft cloth and weight down until the glue dries.

Pad a work surface with a heavy sheet of cardboard. Place sheet of woven straw on the cardboard, straw ribbon side down. With a pencil, trace around the surface of the box or object to be decorated. Use a craft knife to cut around the outline on the sheet of woven straw.

Glue this woven straw design to the box and allow to dry. Trim any overhang with a craft knife.

To protect the straw, apply one of the finishes described in Coloring and Finishing.

surface of the straw (without first coating the straw with the acrylic sealer), it will darken the straw too quickly to shade or highlight.

Natural: Brush glue on the inside (rough) surface of the straw. Allow to dry. Sand the outside (shiny) surface and apply a coat of spray acrylic finish.

PLAITING

There are several terms and techniques basic to plaiting with prepared straw. Before beginning any of the projects involving plaiting, familiarize yourself with the procedures explained below.

Clove Hitch Knot

This is made by securing straw to be woven with two loops of heavy thread tied around a group of straws or dowel. (Diagrams 7a, 7b, and 7c.) Make this knot permanent by tying an overhand knot. (Diagram 8.)

Spiral Weaving

Use a clove hitch knot to attach five straws, heads facing down, to a dowel. Spread straws out with 1 and 2 facing toward you. (Diagram 9a.)

Hold the dowel with your left hand. Fold straw 1 over 2 and 3. Hold on to straw 1 and turn dowel a quarter turn in a clockwise direction. (Diagram 9b.)

Fold straw 3 over 1 and 4. Turn dowel a quarter turn in a clockwise direction. (Diagram 9c.)

Repeat this procedure, moving over two straws at a time. This will form a spiral around the dowel core. (Diagram 9d.) Continue weaving in this manner until the desired length has been reached.

Adding New Straws: When working on a spiral, you will find it necessary to add straws. Insert the slanted end of a straw to the straight or butt end of another straw. (Diagram 10.) Joints are more easily concealed near or under a fold.

Increasing: To increase the width of a spiral, pull straw 1 (or your working straw) slightly to the outside of straw 2. (Diagram 11a.) Straw 2 is now the working straw.

Run it under and over straw 1. Lay straw 2 to the outside of straw 3. (Diagram 11b.) Continue gradually increasing in this manner until reaching desired width.

Decreasing: To decrease the size of spiral, fold straw 1 to the inside of straw 2. (Diagram 12.) Cross straw 2 over straw 1 and to the inside of straw 3.

Four-Straw Plait

Work with four straws of equal length. Holding the straws upside down, tie a clove hitch knot just above the heads. Hold straws between the first and second fingers of the left hand and spread out the straws. (Diagram 13a.) Hold straws in this position with your left thumb. Bend the top straw to the bottom straw. Fold the bottom straw to the top straw position. (Diagram 13b.) Press the folds down with your left thumb.

Fold the right straw to the left straw. Then bend the left straw to the right straw position. Press the folds with your thumb. Continue this process.

Seven-Straw Plait

Holding the straws upside down, tie seven straws together with a clove hitch knot just above the heads. Hold the straws between the first and second fingers of the left hand; then fan out the straws. Working in a clockwise direction, lay straw 1 over straws 2 and 3. Skip one straw (4); then pick up straw 5 and lay it over straws 6 and 7. (Diagram 14.) Skip the next straw, etc. Continue this process, always working in a clockwise direction.

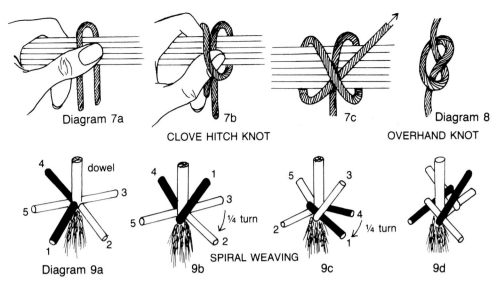

Diagram 7a 7b

CLOVE HITCH KNOT

7c Diagram 8

OVERHAND KNOT

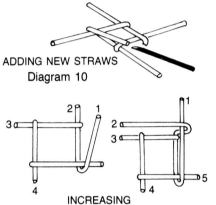

Diagram 9a 9b

SPIRAL WEAVING

9c 9d

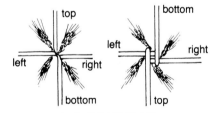

ADDING NEW STRAWS
Diagram 10

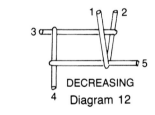

INCREASING

Diagram 11a Diagram 11b

DECREASING

Diagram 12

FOUR-STRAW PLAIT

Diagram 13a Diagram 13b

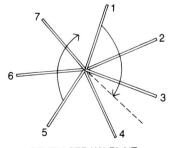

SEVEN-STRAW PLAIT
Diagram 14

Harvest Maiden

It was inevitable in the evolution of the corn dolly that a humanlike figure would emerge. The earliest corn dollies were simple woven spirals, carried aloft at the end of the harvest. Surely if a girl carried the dolly, it was adorned with ribbons and streamers; thus the "harvest maiden" tradition.

The deity of the harvest was always a goddess, either Persephone and Demeter (Greek) or Ceres (Roman). The Harvest Maiden represents the deity in one of two ways, depending upon interpretation: she is either a mother carrying the fruit of the harvest, or she is the maiden bearing seed for the next year's sowing.

Materials
250 stalks of straw (at least 30 should be oat straw with heads, another 50 should be wheat straw with heads)
cream color wax linen thread or similar thread
white household glue
7" cardboard yarn cone (can be made from shirt cardboard)

Equipment
scissors
wallpaper trough, bathtub, or large pan
old bath towel

Prepare straw for plaiting as follows: Using scissors, cut straight across the straw just above the first joint. Pull off any sheath. Place straw in the trough, bathtub, or large pan filled with cold or lukewarm water. Soak for 20 to 30 minutes. Remove straw from the water and roll up in an old towel; leave the straw wrapped in the towel for 15 minutes.

ARMS
Select ten straws without heads, each 11" long. With the linen thread, tie a clove hitch knot 5" in from both ends of these straws. (Diagram 7, page 95.)
Fold the straws ½" from each clove hitch knot to

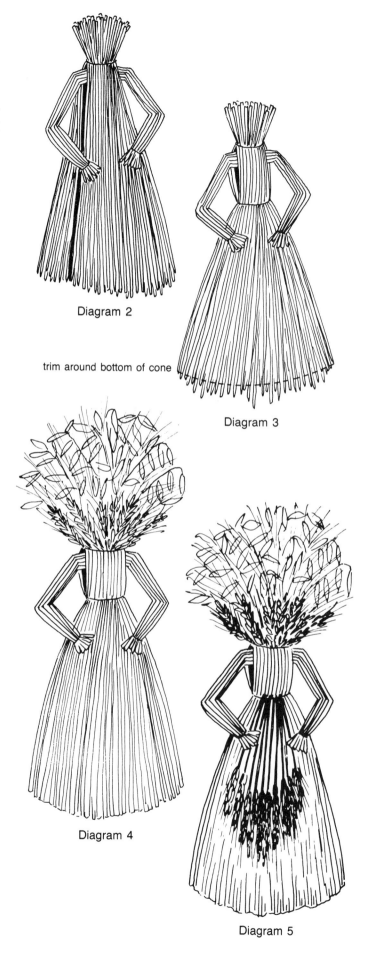

Diagram 2

trim around bottom of cone

Diagram 3

Diagram 4

Diagram 5

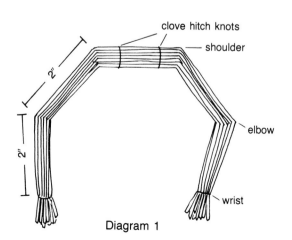

clove hitch knots

shoulder

2'

2'

elbow

wrist

Diagram 1

form the shoulders. Come down 2″ from each shoulder fold and bend the straws to form two elbows. Come down 2″ from both elbows and tie a clove hitch knot to form the wrists. (Diagram 1.) Trim off excess. Set the straw arms aside.

BODY

Gather together seventy-five straws without heads. Come down 2″ from the top and tie a clove hitch knot around the straws to form the neck. Divide the straws in half, insert the arm piece from the bottom of the "skirt" and pull up to the neckline. (Diagram 2.)

Tie a clove hitch knot 2″ down from the neck to form the maiden's waist. (Diagram 3.)

Cover a 7″ cardboard yarn cone with white household glue. Distribute the seventy-five straws of the skirt evenly over the cone and allow the glue to dry. Trim the straws around the bottom of the cone. (Diagram 3.)

Note: If the cone shows through the straws, add more straws, inserting the small end of the straw underneath the outside straws. Work from the bottom of the cone.

HEAD

To form the head of the maiden, choose forty to sixty oat and wheat straws *with heads.* Place half of these straws evenly around the front of the maiden with the heads up and the stalks extending below the bottom of the skirt. (For a "collar" effect around the head, as shown by the Harvest Maiden in the photograph, position the oat straws in the center and distribute the wheat straw with heads around the outside.) Secure the straws in place with a clove hitch knot around the neck. Repeat this procedure on the back of the neck. Tie a clove hitch knot around all the straws at the waistline. (Diagram 4.) Trim the straws again around the bottom of the cone.

APRON

Tie together ten wheat straws with heads. Taper the straws as shown in the photograph so that the center front heads are lower than the heads on the sides of the apron. Place the apron at the front waist of the maiden and tie a clove hitch knot around the waist to secure the apron in place. (Diagram 5.)

FINISHING

Decorate the neck, waist, and skirt bottom of the maiden as desired with different plaits—braiding with three straws, spiral weaving, or four-straw plait. (Diagrams 9-13, page 95.) Tie these plaits with clove hitch knots to each section and glue in place. Allow the glue to dry.

Tie a small bundle of wheat and oats together with a clove hitch knot. Make a spiral weaving using two straws without heads. Tie the spiral to the bundle of wheat and oats with a clove hitch knot. Tie this bundle with a clove hitch knot to the right hand of the maiden. Glue the bundle to the arm and allow to dry.

Geometric Marquetry Box

This box makes use of an inlay look on the top, complemented by weaving on the sides. The straw is treated with wood stain, hand-rubbed for a patina of age. An intriguing study of textures, this box is a welcome addition to any collection of straw work, boxes, or desk-top or table items.

Materials

oat straw	tracing paper
2¾″-square box	acrylic sealer
acrylic paint	water-base wood stain
white household glue	polyurethane finish

Equipment

scissors	pencil
bathtub, or large pan	ruler
old towel	cardboard
paintbrush	craft knife
seam ripper	sandpaper
iron	sponge brush
soft cloth	

Follow the instructions in Preparing the Straw (page 93).

Paint the inside of the cardboard box and lid and the side of the box that will be covered by the lid with acrylic paint.

Split the straw according to instructions in Preparing the Straw Ribbon (page 93).

Cut out the design for the top of the lid following the pattern shown here and cut straw ribbons in 3″ lengths to fit all four sides of the lid. (See paragraphs 1 through 3 in Working with Straw Ribbons, page 93.)

Follow paragraphs 1 through 4 in Woven Straw Work (page 94) for all four sides of the box, cutting ¼″-wide straw ribbons to be woven in the vertical direction and ⅛″-wide ribbons for the horizontal direction, as shown in the photograph. Cut the prepared straw sheet so that it fits just under the bottom of the lid. This will ensure easy closure and removal of the lid.

Glue prepared straw sheets to the box and allow to dry. Following the instructions for Water-Base Wood Stain under Coloring and Finishing the Straw Ribbon (page 94), apply a coat of acrylic sealer to the box and allow to dry. Using the sponge brush, apply wood stain to the entire outside surface of the box. Wipe off excess stain with a soft cloth; allow to dry.

Complete by applying a polyurethane finish, using as many coats as necessary. Allow to dry.

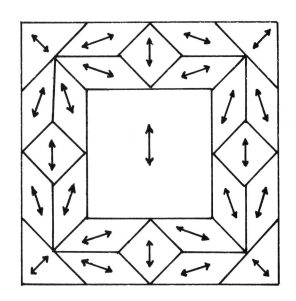

Sunflower Box

This project is a fine introduction to straw marquetry and to the methods of coloring straw. The bright, transparent colors are achieved with glass stain—a perfect choice because it allows the texture of the straw to show through. The repetition of two simple shapes—a petal and a circle—is a very effective design. Plan to make several at one time; they make cheerful, cherished gifts.

Materials
oat straw
round wooden box, preferably with a beveled top
water-base wood stain
acrylic paint in yellow and brown
white household glue
tracing paper
glass stain in yellow and brown
glass stain thinner
polyurethane finish

Equipment
scissors	sandpaper
bathtub or large pan	sponge brush
towel	small paintbrush
seam ripper	soft cloth
iron	hole punch

Follow the instructions in Preparing the Straw (page 93). Then split the straw according to the instructions in Preparing the Straw Ribbon (page 93).

Sand the wooden box. Using the sponge brush, apply a thin coat of water-base wood stain over the entire box. Wipe off the excess stain and allow the box to dry. Paint the trim around the top of the lid and around the bottom of the box with yellow acrylic paint. Allow the paint to dry; then paint the inside of the box yellow with brown polka dots. Allow to dry.

Follow the instructions in the first paragraph of Working with Straw Ribbons under Marquetry (page 93). Make two sheets of straw ribbons, one for the petals and one for the centers of the flowers. Paint one straw ribbon sheet with yellow glass stain and the other with brown glass stain; allow to dry.

Make a tracing of the petals from the pattern given here, following the arrows for the direction of the straw. Follow the instructions in paragraphs 3 and 4 of Working with Straw Ribbons (page 94) with the yellow sheet of straw ribbons.

With a hole punch, punch out circles for the center of the flower from the brown sheet of straw ribbons.

Glue the yellow petals onto the top of the wooden box first; then glue the brown centers in place and allow the glue to dry. Apply a protective finish of polyurethane and allow to dry.

Join the plaited end just above the heads of the straw with a clove hitch knot. Trim off any excess unplaited straw with scissors. With the grosgrain ribbon, tie a bow around the clove hitch knot just above the heads of straw.

Love Token

Materials
24 stalks of straw (wheat or barley)
cream color wax linen or similar thread,
18″ narrow grosgrain ribbon
white household glue

Equipment
scissors
wallpaper trough, bathtub, or large pan
old bath towel

Prepare the straw for plaiting as follows: With scissors, cut straight across the straw just above the first joint. Pull off any sheath. Place the straw in the wallpaper trough, bathtub, or large pan filled with cold or lukewarm water. Soak the straw for 20 to 30 minutes. Remove the straw from the water and roll up in an old towel; leave the straw wrapped in the towel for 15 minutes.

Remove seven straws from the towel. (Leave remaining seventeen straws in the towel until needed.) Hold the straws upside down; then, with linen thread, tie a clove hitch knot just above the heads. (Diagram 7, page 95.) Make this knot permanent by tying an overhand knot. (Diagram 8, page 95.)

Beginning just above the heads, braid the straw for 5″ using the Seven-Straw Plait. (Diagram 14, page 95.) Tie a clove hitch knot with thread at the end of the plaiting. Trim down unplaited straw to ½″.

Repeat the above steps with seven more straws for the other half of the heart.

Join the two halves of the heart together with clove hitch knots. Tie above the heads of the straw and at the end of the plaiting.

Remove the remaining ten straws from the towel. Divide the straws into two groups of five straws each. Place five straws on top of the front side and five straws on the back side of the heart. Tie the straws in place with a clove hitch knot around the heads.

Shape the plaiting, keeping it round at the top of the heart. Tie a clove hitch knot above and below the plaiting to secure the heart shape.

Measure 1″ above the top of the heart and cut the straw stalks off at an angle.

Using 6″ of ribbon, criss-cross it around the top of the heart and tie off in an overhand knot. Glue the knot and allow to dry. Cut off any excess ribbon. Tie a bow around the bottom of the heart using 12″ of ribbon.

Countryman's Favor

Materials
7 stalks of straw (wheat or barley)
cream color wax linen thread or similar thread
6″ narrow grosgrain ribbon

Equipment
scissors
wallpaper trough, bathtub, or large pan
old bath towel

Prepare straw for plaiting as follows: Using scissors, cut straight across the straw just above the first joint. Pull off any sheath. Place straw in the trough, bathtub, or large pan filled with cold or lukewarm water. Soak for 20 to 30 minutes. Remove the straw from the water and roll up in an old towel; leave the straw wrapped in the towel for 15 minutes.

Remove the seven straws from the towel. Hold the straws upside down; then, using thread, tie a clove hitch knot just above the heads. (Diagram 7, page 95.) Make this knot permanent by tying an overhand knot. (Diagram 8, page 95.)

Beginning just above the heads, braid the straw for 5″ using the Seven-Straw Plait. (Diagram 14, page 95.) Tie a clove hitch knot with thread at the end of the plaiting.

WinterCrafts

Snow Personalities

When the classic snowman originated, someone used what was on hand to suggest a personality. That same practical innovation can introduce new characters to your neighborhood.

Think of dressing your winter visitors with the same inventiveness you used as a child when playing dress-up in Mother's discards. A summer tablecloth and napkins of Polynesian batik sparked the idea for the Island Lady "Snow-She" shown here. Fruit from the refrigerator made a colorful lei when threaded onto florist's wire, and "Carmen Miranda" earrings were pinned on with toothpicks.

Pine cones left over from Christmas decorations made a fashionable, curly bob on the front yard character shown on the preceding page. The pine cones were secured on florist's picks (Diagram 1, page 128), and the picks were stuck into the snow. A broccoli cluster turned this snow creature into a green-eyed beauty, and spruce was trimmed into an extravagant eyelash. Betty Boop never had a prettier pout than these lips cut from orange peel.

The winter landscape holds many imaginative decorations, so don't limit your search to the house. Press red berries into soft snow for lips and fashion hair from holly leaves for a Christmas snow hostess. You could layer clusters of pine needles for straight hair and a beard or use vines to suggest hair.

The classic snowman shape is three balls in graduating sizes. Female figures benefit from slight sculpting. The suggestion of a skirt at the bottom and an uplifted bosom are more appealing than a roly-poly lady.

Once you begin surveying accessories in your closets and kitchen cabinets, you will discover an unlimited number of unique possibilities. A little originality often spawns a neighborhood competition.

Snow Angels

The only equipment you need to make snow angels is warm clothing, but there is a special talent required—you must be a strong jumper. Once you've spread an angel silhouette in the snow, you must jump as far as possible away from the angel so that earthly footprints won't interfere with her flight.

Jump first, as far as you can, into clear snow and lie down face up in a spread-eagle position. The rest is simple; move your arms and legs back and forth to clear snow from the angel's wings and skirts. Then stand up and jump out. Hallelujah!

Icicle City

It's hard to match a child's spontaneous creativity. Icicle City was born when a restless six-year-old became fascinated with the icicles that grew long in the late months of winter. He collected the biggest icicles he could find and put them upside down in several inches of snow, observing an urban block pattern and reproducing the skyscrapers of his city. Matchbox trucks came next, and his winter environment was complete. There's even a cloud of crusty snow caught on one of the skyscrapers.

Sean, the designer of the city shown here, found his icicles on a greenhouse, where they are particularly long and, in his case, low enough for him to reach. If there's not a greenhouse near you, wait for the first warming thaw in March when all icicles grow longer. Then check a protected corner of your house for the longest ones of all.

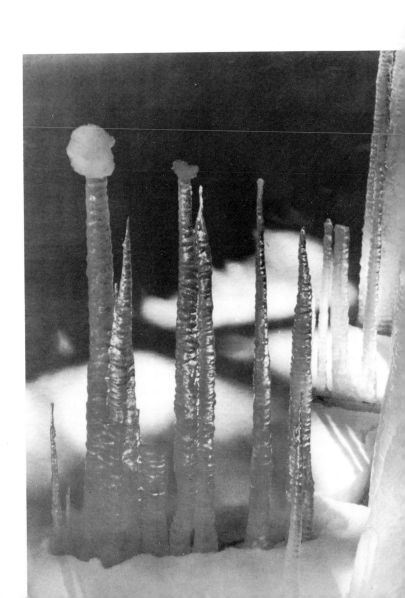

Snow Lanterns

Snow lanterns are a wonderful, northern variation of the Mexican luminaries, which have spread in popularity at Christmastime. The lanterns are a festive welcome at Christmas or for any winter entertaining. A single lantern is a delightful surprise for guests, and several lining your walk or drive can be very dramatic. It's a good job for children—if you can stop them from throwing every snowball they make.

Make firm snowballs about the size of softballs. One lantern requires about 27 snowballs. Place votive (or plumber's) candles in the snow along the walk and stack the snowballs around each candle in a pyramid form.

Use long matches to light the candles quickly at just the last minute, since the lanterns cannot, unfortunately, last for long. They'll last longer, however, if you leave off the top snowball of the pyramid. (The top ball sits directly over the candle; it soon melts and snuffs the light.)

Ice Panels

On snowy winter days when excitement deteriorates to "What can we do?", ice panels are a delightful pastime—easy enough for children, beautiful for several days, and free. Hanging in the bare trees, they twist in the wind, adding color and sparkle to the winter landscape.

Materials

pie pans	berries
water	evergreen
yarn	flowers

Fill a pie pan with water and line the edge of the pan with yarn. Leave enough yarn loose at the top to tie around a tree branch. Gather greenery and berries and arrange them in the water. Include the fading blossoms from a dinner party centerpiece; in ice, the blooms retain their color and look fresh again. Find other bits of color in house plants that need cutting back or from an old bowl of potpourri.

Put the pans on a flat surface outside until the water freezes and the yarn and flowers are locked in ice. If you have trouble removing the ice panel from the pan, dip it in warm water as you would to remove gelatin from a mold.

For a more spectacular display, make several ice panels at once using loaf pans and plastic drawer-organizers as molds; then hang the different shapes together. Sun on the ice creates unique winter beauty and sparkle, and the ice panels will last as long as the temperatures stay below freezing. Even if the temperatures are above freezing during the day, the ice panels will stay pretty for two or three days.

Spice Necklaces

Wearing a spice necklace is like wearing jewelry and perfume in one. Body heat intensifies the rich, warm scent of these necklaces. Stringing the spices onto fishing line is quick and easy, although puncturing a hole in some of the spices requires real engineering.

Materials
cinnamon sticks
whole cloves
whole allspice
cardamom
frankincense (translucent yellow resin)
star anise
whole nutmeg
clay or wooden beads (optional)
transparent fishing line
jewelry fasteners

Equipment
sewing needle
thimble
small blow torch or gas range
pliers
vise
electric drill with smallest bit

Break cinnamon sticks into small pieces. Soak cloves, allspice, and cinnamon sticks in warm water for 12 to 24 hours; they will then be soft enough to push a needle through with a thimble. (Cardamom is soft enough to pierce without soaking.)

Burn a hole in the frankincense and star anise by heating a needle with a blow torch or over the flame of a gas range. Use pliers to hold the needle in the flame; then push the hot needle (still held with pliers) through the spice. Repeat until the hole is burned through.

Secure nutmeg in a vise and drill a hole with a small drill bit.

Lay the spices out in a preliminary design. If you study the necklaces shown here, you'll see that the star anise makes a distinctive pendant in the center. Concentrate the cloves and cinnamon sticks, which are strung crosswise, near the pendant, or center, and use round allspice at the ends of the necklace where they will be in contact with the wearer's neck. Clay or wooden beads are a nice contrast to the spices.

A finished necklace of 36″ is the most attractive hanging length. Cut the fishing line in lengths of 48″, allowing 6″ at each end to attach the fasteners.

Thread the fishing line through a sewing needle and slide the pendant, or center spice, on first. Complete one full 18″ side of the necklace. Then remove the needle and thread it with the opposite end of the fishing line. Using the finished side as a pattern, duplicate the same design on the opposite side of the necklace.

On each end, pull the needle around the outside of the last spice and then back through the hole in the end spice again. Tie a knot as closely as possible to the end spice to prevent gaps in the necklace.

Tie one end of the line onto a male fastener and the other end onto a female fastener. Secure with a knot and trim the excess line.

GOURDS:
Clowns of the Plant Kingdom

No one knows exactly when or where mankind first recognized the gourd's potential as a vessel, utensil, and musical instrument, but as early as 7000 B.C., the bottle gourd was in use in Mexico. Decorated gourd containers and musical instruments have been used for centuries and are still being used today in Africa, Asia, New Zealand, Hawaii, and South America. Many of the designs you see here are adaptations of very early ornamental patterns when, with an enviable naïveté, primitive artists let each individual shape determine the use and decoration of the gourd.

Many of the decorating techniques still in use today had their origin in primitive cultures. Pyrography (burned designs), cutting, carving, and coloring have changed little; however, the tools used are often quite dissimilar, designs differ, and coloring and staining materials in most areas have changed from dyes made from natural materials to commercially produced paints and stains.

The gourd projects presented here represent techniques used throughout the world. Gourds are worked with tools and processes similar to those used for working, shaping, and decorating wood—chip carving, woodburning, painting, staining, decoupage, and tole painting, for example.

There are two general types of gourds. Ornamental gourds (*cucurbita pepo*) are closely related to the many varieties of edible squash. These gourds have large yellow flowers and small, often brightly colored, fruit. Their growing season is relatively short. Ornamental gourds should be harvested before frost and cured for about three months.

Hard-shell or calabash gourds (*Lagenaria spp.*) have a longer growing season and a curing time

of six months to one year. The calabash gourd has white flowers and thick-shelled fruit which can be small or quite large and which are not damaged by light frost.

TERMS

It is helpful if you are familiar with a few of the terms involved in working with gourds.

Outer skin: Outside surface of the gourd, often brightly colored on ornamentals. (This skin is removed and discarded while cleaning.)

Rind: Tough, cream-colored or brown layer beneath the outer skin. The rind is water-resistant and difficult to carve, cut, or dye.

Pith: Layer just beneath the gourd rind. It is lighter in color, softer, and easier to dye or carve.

Inner skin: Soft, spongy lining of gourd, containing seeds. (This skin is removed and discarded while cleaning.)

Curing: Allowing gourds (after reaching maturity) to become hard and light in weight through proper drying procedures.

Cleaning: Removing both outer skin and inner skin by alternately soaking in water and scraping with a sharp instrument.

CURING

Gourds can be harvested when rinds are hard and the gourds have begun to dry on the vine and have become light in weight. To harvest, cut the stem from the vine, handling the gourd carefully to avoid bruising. Gently wash the gourd in a non-bleaching disinfectant and store in a warm, airy place out of the sun to dry. Complete drying or curing may take three months for ornamentals and six months to a year for calabash gourds. Calabashes may cure in the field and are not affected by the frost in the mild winter areas, but ornamentals should be dried under frost-free conditions. While curing, all varieties may develop patches of unsightly mold, but these will be removed along with the outer skin while cleaning.

Ornamentals can be quick-dried in about one week indoors in winter. Drill a small hole in one or both ends and place the gourd over a forced-air heater vent. Turn the gourd daily for even drying.

You can order gourd seeds to grow your own, or you can order gourds that have already been dried and cured. (See Suppliers, page 150.) Unfortunately, the ornamental gourds that look so inviting in the grocery store are usually waxed, and the wax seal prevents normal drying so that these gourds will deteriorate after one season. While they are appealing for fall decorations, they do not have the permanence you would want before investing your time in gourd projects such as those shown here.

MICROWAVE CURING

Small gourds can be quickly cured in a microwave oven using a mixture of equal parts silica gel and sand. The microwave not only reduces the curing time, but it makes possible some decorations that are not feasible without rapid curing. For instance, it is much easier to scratch-carve a design (a shallow cut through only the outer skin and rind) while the gourd is green, or freshly picked, because after several months of curing, the rind becomes very tough and hard to cut. However, if you scratch-carve or pierce a green gourd and then leave it to cure, the carved areas will curl inward, distorting the shape of the gourd.

Uncured gourds can be green-carved or green-stained but must be quickly dried in the microwave oven in order to retain their shape. When properly dried in the microwave oven, the outer skin need not be removed.

Caution: Some manufacturers do not recommend drying gourds in their microwave ovens; check with the manufacturer of your model before you proceed.

Freshly picked gourds have a high water content and must be handled according to the following rules to prevent their bursting in the microwave oven: 1) Always drill vent holes and leave these unobstructed during cooking. 2) Allow gourds to cool naturally in the microwave oven. 3) Adjust cooking time when processing two or more gourds. 4) Place a cup of water in the microwave oven with the gourds and check the level of the water frequently.

Select smooth, ripe ornamental gourds. Drill a ¼"-diameter "vent" hole to the center of the gourd from both the blossom and the stem ends to allow moisture to escape while cooking.

Carve and/or stain gourds before heating in the microwave. Place the gourd on a bed of equal parts sand and silica gel in a casserole, making sure the vents in the gourd are unobstructed. (Diagram 1.) Consult the manufacturer's cooking instructions for the correct timing to bake winter squash, but you will not "cook" the gourd in one continuous cycle. With the gourd on the silica gel mixture, heat for 2 or 3 minutes only. Allow the gourd to cool completely inside the oven.

When the gourd has cooled, open the oven and turn the gourd on the silica gel mixture. (Eventually, all areas of the outside of the gourd should come in contact with the silica gel mixture.) Make sure the vents are unobstructed and heat again for 2 or 3 minutes. Let cool and turn the gourd before reheating.

Continue a cycle of heating, cooling, and turning the gourd until the total cooking time is equal to the manufacturer's recommended time for baking winter squash. These short cycles will remove moisture safely and grad-

ually while cooking the interior.

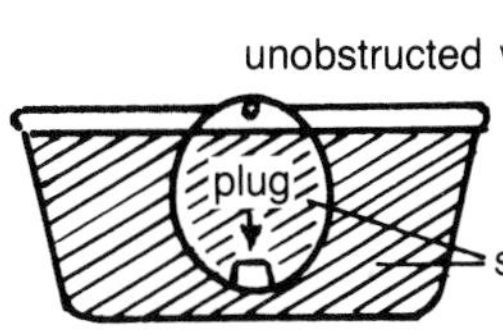

When the interior is cooked and soft, cut a ½"-square plug from 1 end and scrape the pulp and seeds from the interior wall of the gourd. Remove the contents of the gourd through the plug and save the plug.

Fill the empty gourd with additional silica gel and sand mixture to hasten drying and to prevent the gourd from collapsing. Replace the plug and invert the gourd. Leaving the top vent unobstructed, bury the gourd in the silica gel mixture in the casserole. (Diagram 2.) Continue heating for 2-minute cycles and cooling inside the oven until the gourd is tough and light in weight.

When dry, empty the silica gel mixture from the gourd and gently brush mixture from the carved areas. Replace the plug.

CLEANING

The outer skin can be removed during curing as soon as it can be easily scraped off. As an alternative method, remove the skin after curing by wrapping the gourd in a wet terry towel for about 1 hour to soften the outer skin, and then scrape the skin away with a dull knife or the edge of a spoon.

After removing the outer skin, you may find the rind stained by mold markings. These can be concealed by burned finishes, paints, or dyes as described in Coloring and Finishing. When using quick-drying methods, mold may not develop.

After a gourd is cut open, as described for three of the projects that follow, soak it for 1 hour in a basin of water to soften the inner skin; then scrape with a spoon to separate the inner skin from the pith. (Soaking overnight in a solution of baking soda and water should remove the bitter taste from gourds you plan to use as food containers.) After the cleaned gourd has dried, heat a conventional oven to 300° F.; then turn the oven off and place the gourd inside until the oven cools. This will remove moisture and improve carving qualities.

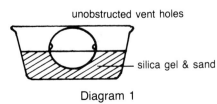

unobstructed vent holes

silica gel & sand

Diagram 1

unobstructed vent hole

plug

silica gel & sand

Diagram 2

CUTTING, SAWING, AND CARVING GOURDS

Green Gourds

Green, or freshly picked, gourds can be easily cut and decorated before curing and drying. A V-shaped linoleum gouge, pushed with a rocking motion, chips a deep channel through the rind and into the pith. A craft knife with a straight or curved blade can be used to engrave a clean line with one cut or to carve a V-shaped channel with two parallel opposing cuts. Leather hole punches and tooling stamps will imprint a freshly picked gourd, and the point of an awl will make delicate line patterns.

All cuts into the pith of a green gourd will readily absorb water or solvent-based leather dyes and other coloring agents. The longer the interval between cutting and dyeing green gourds, the lighter the color will be. These gourds should be dried as rapidly as possible after decorating, preferably with a microwave oven or in silica gel.

Although gourds can be quickly and easily carved while green, the edges of the cuts will tend to curl inward during drying. Cutting lids or deeply incised patterns should therefore be postponed as long as possible, preferably until curing is complete. The path of a cut can be incised by one of the surface carving methods suggested above; then the cut can be completed after the gourd is fully cured.

Cured Gourds

Fully cured gourds have an extremely tough rind, which is much more difficult to carve than the green gourds using the hand tools mentioned above. Tools tend to skid over the smooth surface of the cured gourd and into the hand holding the gourd. Use a downward rather than a forward pressure when working with these gourds, tape the hand holding the gourd, and sharpen your tools frequently.

Electric drills, saws, and mo-torized tools are very useful for carving or cutting cured gourds. Protective goggles and a dust mask are essential when using these tools, and a vise is helpful for holding the gourd in place so that both hands are free for guiding the tool.

COLORING AND FINISHING

Toasting

Gourds can be burned, dyed, glazed, painted, and coated with protective finishes to improve their appearance and to help preserve them.

Mold colonies that form on the outer skin during the curing process may discolor the rind in irregular patterns. If these patterns are objectionable, the rind may be darkened. Lightly oil and then toast the gourd one or more times in a conventional oven heated to 300° F. and then turned off before the gourd is placed inside.

Broiling

Discolored gourds may be darkened rapidly by holding the oiled gourd over a stove burner which has been turned to its highest setting. Hold the gourd about 2" above the burner, turning it constantly until it is evenly browned. Small ornamental gourds can be skewered on an aluminum afghan hook to avoid having your hand too close to the heat.

Note: Protect the hand holding the gourd with an oven mitt or protective glove. Keep a container of water handy in which to submerge the gourd should it catch fire.

Torching

A propane torch can be used to produce either a mottled pattern or a burned, even browning of the rind. A woodburning tool can be used to draw designs.

Pigments

The rind is tough, smooth, and water-resistant, but seems to absorb oils and solvent-based pigments; the pith will accept both water- and solvent-based pig-ments. Carved gourds can be stained with water-based dyes to produce a dark, carved pattern against a tinted background, or several applications of solvent-based dyes can give a deep, rich color to the rind.

Gourds should be lightly sanded to improve adhesion of paints. Apply a base coat of enamel under-body before finishing the gourd with enamel paint. And apply an acrylic polymer medium before applying acrylic artist's paints.

Use glass stains for transparent colors that are especially nice for an antiqued effect on carved gourds.

Sealing

Painted surfaces should be protected by a coat of clear varnish, polyurethane, or an acrylic polymer medium.

Finish oiled gourds with a coat of paste wax.

If a gourd is to be used as a container, waterproof it by "painting" the inside with melted paraffin. This will prevent liquid from seeping through the rind.

Caution: Heat paraffin in a double boiler.

TRANSFERRING AND MARKING DESIGNS

Designs for carving, woodburning, or painting gourds can be transferred in a number of ways. Light pencil marks are usually sufficient to indicate pattern or placement and can easily be erased when no longer needed. A stencil or tracing paper can be used to transfer simple repeats. Geometric designs are marked with a compass or an improvised compass made with a push pin, string, and a pencil. (Diagram 3.)

To locate the equator of the gourd, position a compass so that the pointed end is secured at the blossom scar on the base of the gourd. Measure the distance from the blossom scar to the stem scar, divide by two, and adjust the arm of the compass to transcribe a circle with this radius. Place the pencil end against the side of the gourd with the point still at the stem end, and make a line all the way around the gourd. This is the equator. (Diagram 3.)

Cut a piece of string to fit around the circumference of the gourd at the equator line. Fold the string to divide it into the required number of equal segments. (Fold the string in half to divide it into two equal parts or into fourths, etc.) Mark the fold lines with penciled dots on the string to indicate the dividing line between segments. Place the string around the equator and transfer the marks on the string to the gourd.

Additional geometric divisions can be made with the compass once the equator has been marked, measured, and divided into segments. Motifs for the projects in this section are also shown below.

The Dark Brown Pierced Pomander (page 114) was marked to divide it into two segments at the equator. The compass was adjusted to draw a circle with a diameter of slightly less than one segment. The point was placed at a mark on the equator, and a circle was drawn. This was repeated for the other side. Each of the two resulting ovals was filled with a variation of the eight-pointed star shown here.

For the Light Brown Pierced Pomander (page 113), the Green Carved Ornament (page 115), and the Clove-Studded Pomander (page 116), the equator was divided into four segments. The arm of the compass was set for a diameter slightly less than two segments in the two pomanders, and slightly more than two segments in the ornament. Four circles were drawn using the marks on the equator as compass pivot points (Diagram 4.)

For the Woodburned Ornament (page 112), the equator was divided into five segments, and the arm of the compass set for a diameter of two segments, with five circles drawn.

The point of the compass can be set just above the equator, as on the Light Brown Pierced Pomander, or just below it, as on the Woodburned Ornament. Additional circles can be drawn parallel to the equator to produce hori-

zontal bands as on the Light Brown Pierced Pomander and the Green Carved Ornament.

The geometric motifs given here are shown in closeup photographs of the gourd pomanders and ornaments that appear on pages 112-116. But don't let these designs limit your imagination. Often, the most distinctive designs are those you create freehand.

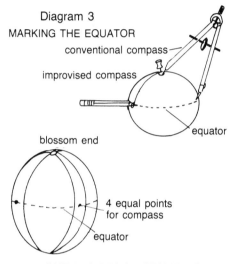

Diagram 3
MARKING THE EQUATOR
conventional compass
improvised compass
equator
blossom end
4 equal points for compass
equator

MARKING DESIGN SEGMENTS
Diagram 4

MOTIFS SUGGESTED FOR CARVING GOURD POMANDERS AND ORNAMENTS (pages 112-116)
Solid lines are motif lines. Broken lines are grid lines.

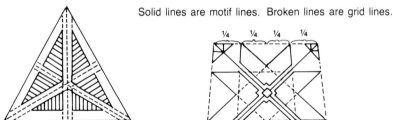

Triangle for Woodburned Ornament

Star for Light Brown Pierced Pomander

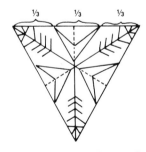

Triangle for Light Brown Pierced Pomander

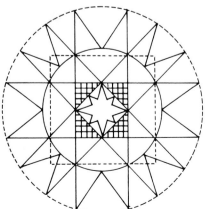

Star for Dark Brown Pierced Pomander

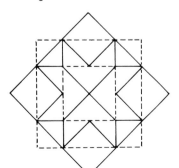

Star for Green Carved Ornament

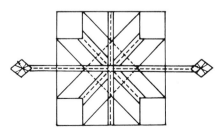

Star for Clove Studded Pomander

Gourd Thumb Piano

The *Kalimba*, or thumb piano, comes from Africa where its use is widespread. Considering the range and power of its sound, it is unusually portable. Its metal tongues may be played with the thumbs, fingers, or mallets, and a vibrato effect can be produced by covering and uncovering the two holes in the sides of the gourd while striking a note.

The metal tongues are tuned by pushing them toward (raises pitch) or away from (lowers pitch) the bridge.

Various techniques and tunings can be developed by playing and experimenting. One can use major or minor scales for different sounds. Diagram 1 shows a major scale with "C" as the first and lowest note.

An easy playing technique is to play notes on the left side, (2, 4, 6, 8) with the left thumb and notes on the right side (1, 3, 5, 7) with the right thumb. Using the major scale illustrated, the melody to "Mary Had a Little Lamb" could be played as follows:

3212333 222 355 3212333 322321

Clean the gourd portion with furniture polish and polish the metal tongues and bridge with fine steel wool. A light application of oil or furniture polish will keep rust off the metal tongues and bridge.

Complete bridge kits in various key widths can be ordered through the mail. (See Suppliers, page 150.) Or, you can make your own bridge and key assembly by following the instructions given here.

Materials
smooth calabash gourd (*Lagenaria spp.*) with minimum of ¼"-thick walls, cured and cleaned
varnish or acrylic spray
¼"-thick piece hardwood
scrap piece hardwood
wood glue

3½"-long piece ⅜"-diameter rod stock (hot-rolled)
2 (1¼"-long) 6-32 round head machine screws with T-nuts
metal/wood cement (optional)
grass rake with spring metal tines
44"-long piece rawhide cord
3½"-long piece ⅛"-diameter brass welding rod
Danish oil

Equipment
fine-tooth handsaw or saber saw
sandpaper
spoon
pencil
electric drill with 9/64", 3/16", and 5/8" bits and 1½" hole saw
metalworking file
center punch
vise
hacksaw
screwdriver

Cut the gourd in half with a hand or saber saw and smooth the cut edge with sandpaper. Soak the bottom half in water for 1 hour or more. Remove the outer skin and both the seeds and the inner skin with a spoon. Allow the gourd to dry completely. Coat the inside of the gourd to seal it, using either varnish or acrylic spray.

Turn the gourd cut side down and trace the outline of the gourd with a pencil onto the ¼"-thick piece of hardwood. (Mahogany was used for the thumb piano pictured here.) With a saw, cut out the shape traced onto the wood for the top of the instrument.

Cut the wooden bridge 3½" × 1⅜" × ½" from a scrap piece of hardwood such as mahogany or cherry.

Cut one groove ⅜" wide x ⅛" deep in the wooden bridge for the metal bridge and the rawhide cord. Cut a shallow (1/16"-deep) notch for the brass rod. (Diagram 2.)

Attach the wooden bridge to the hardwood top with wood glue. Make sure you position the bridge perpendicular to the grain of the hardwood top and slightly off-center with the wide groove closer to the outside edge of the top.

With the hole saw, cut a 1½"-diameter sound hole in the hardwood top of the gourd, positioning it so that the center of the hole is 1¾" from the edge of the bridge. (Diagram 1.)

Smooth the ends of the piece of rod stock with a metalworking file. With the center punch, mark two holes in the metal bridge 1¾" apart. Secure the

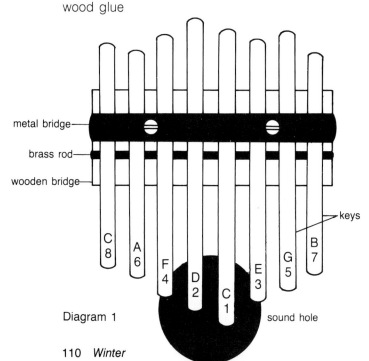

metal bridge ———
brass rod ———
wooden bridge ———

keys

C 8 A 6 F 4 D 2 C 1 E 3 G 5 B 7

Diagram 1   sound hole

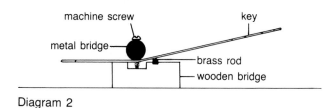

machine screw   key
metal bridge ———
                       brass rod
                       wooden bridge

Diagram 2

bridge in a vise and drill holes using the 9/64″ drill bit.

With the metal bridge as a guide, mark corresponding holes in the large groove in the wooden bridge. Drill the holes in the wooden bridge through the hardwood top, using the 3/16″ drill bit.

Turn the top over and firmly tap one T-nut into each drilled hole. (Since it is important that the T-nuts stay in position while you complete the bridge assembly, you may wish to add a small dab of metal/wood cement around each T-nut.)

Turn the top right side up and glue the top to the gourd with wood glue. Allow to dry; then use sandpaper to smooth the edges and remove excess glue.

Drill two ⅝″-diameter vibrato holes on opposite sides of the gourd, roughly on a straight line with the front edge of the bridge and so that the center of each hole is 1¾″ below the top edge of the piano.

Select a grass rake with tines that correspond in width to the diameter of your piano top. (See chart.)

Cut a few tines from the garden rake with the hacksaw. Clamp a tine in a vise with the correct length of metal extending above the jaws of the vise. Use Diagram 1 as a guide to the key lengths. (The lengths are approximate, however, because the only part of the key that affects the sound is what extends *over* the sound hole. But you do want to make the keys long enough so you can tune your piano.)

Bend the metal sharply against the vise to snap/break a length of metal off. Repeat the procedure until you have eight keys. Round and smooth the ends of each key with the metalworking file.

Lay the rawhide cord in the wide groove in the wooden bridge. Place the metal bridge in the same groove. Insert machine screws through the holes and start into the nuts below. Lay the brass welding rod in the small notch. (The tension of the keys will hold the rod in place.) Slip the keys under the metal bridge and adjust for correct tones. Tighten the screws with a screwdriver.

Note: It is important that you tighten the screws through the metal and wooden bridges *after* the top is firmly glued to the gourd. If you reverse the assembly order, the pressure of tightening the screws may distort the shape of the top and prevent it from properly fitting the gourd.

Clean the piano and rub with Danish oil. Tie a knot in the ends of the rawhide cord, slip the cord around your neck so that the keys of the piano face toward you, and begin to play!

Hardwood Top Diameter	Key Width
4″ to 6″ (small)	1/8″
6″ to 8″ (medium)	3/16″
over 8″ (large)	1/4″

(Left to right): Green Carved Ornament, Dark Brown Pierced Pomander, Woodburned Ornament, Light Brown Pierced Pomander, and Clove-Studded Ornament.

Woodburned Ornament

Materials
ornamental gourd, cured and cleaned, with no
   surface discoloration
wooden bead
2 skeins embroidery floss
white household glue

Equipment
compass
string
pencil
woodburning tool
hand or electric drill with small bit
artist's knife with #11 blade
lightweight cardboard

Following the instructions and the motif in Transferring and Marking Designs (page 108), mark the equator of the gourd with a compass. With string, divide the gourd into five equal segments and mark these segments on the equator line. With the point of the compass on one mark, adjust the pencil arm so that it coincides with the next adjacent mark. Draw a circle of that radius at each of the five marks.

Following the manufacturer's directions for using the woodburning tool, trace over all marked pattern lines (page 109) with smooth, even strokes.

Drill small holes at each end of the gourd for inserting the hanging cord and tassel. With the artist's knife, cut a ½"-square plug in the bottom and reserve the plug.

Make a tassel and assemble the ornament as described for the Light Brown Pierced Pomander (page 113), omitting the spices.

Light Brown Pierced Pomander

Materials
ornamental gourd, cured and cleaned
water-base leather dye
2 skeins embroidery floss
wooden bead
assorted whole spices
paste wax
white household glue

Equipment
electric drill with ¼'' bit
compass
string
pencil
linoleum-cutting tool with V-shaped gouge
artist's knife with #11 blade
soft cloth
lightweight cardboard

Drill ¼'' holes in each end of the gourd.

Following the instructions and the motif in Transferring and Marking Designs (page 108), mark the equator of the gourd with a compass. With string, divide the equator into four equal segments and mark these points on the equator line. Adjust the compass arm so that the diameter will be slightly smaller than two segments (or one-half of the gourd).

With the point of the compass at each mark on the equator, draw four circles.

Use a linoleum-cutting tool with a V-shaped gouge to incise all the pattern lines (page 109). Push with a rocking motion to chip a deep channel through the rind and into the pith. (Practice cutting on a scrap gourd and sharpen your tool often.)

Cut a ½''-square plug from the bottom of the gourd and save the plug. Use an artist's knife to cut all the way through the openwork areas as shown in the photograph and discard these pieces. Points on the stars are fragile and may break from the pressure of the knife blade. If this happens, carefully glue the piece back in place.

When carving is complete, stain the gourd with a solution of equal parts water-base leather dye and water. Brush the stain on with a soft cloth and allow to set for 30 seconds; then wipe off. Allow to dry. Coat gourd with paste wax and buff with a soft cloth.

TASSEL
Cut a 24'' length of embroidery floss and put aside for the hanger.

Wind the remaining floss around a 4'' by 6'' piece of cardboard. Wind around the 4'' width for a 4'' tassel and around the 6'' length for a 6'' tassel. (Diagram 1.)

Slip one end of the 24'' hanger under the tassel loops and tie tightly in a knot. Cut the opposite ends of the loops and separate strands to fluff the tassel.

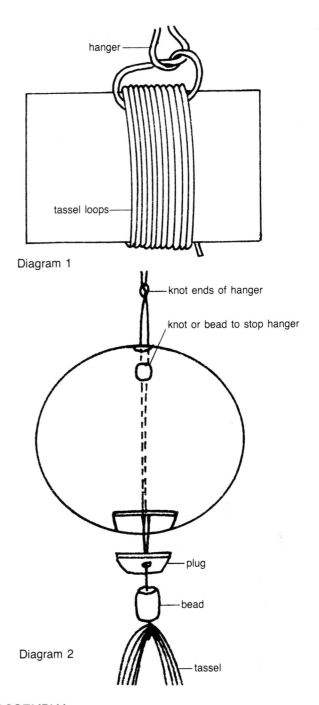

Diagram 1

Diagram 2

ASSEMBLY
Slide the wooden bead onto the double hanger thread so that it rests just above the tassel. Drill a small hole in the center of the square plug and slide it onto the hanger thread so that the inside of the plug faces up. (Diagram 2)

Measure from the plug a length on the hanger thread equal to the length of the gourd and tie a large knot at that spot or slightly below, toward the plug. Thread the hanger through the gourd as shown and tie the ends of the hanger in a square knot.

Turn the gourd upside down and fill half-full with mixed whole spices. Glue the plug into place and let dry.

Dark Brown Pierced Pomander

Materials
ornamental gourd, cured and cleaned
cooking oil
2 skeins embroidery floss
wooden bead
assorted whole spices—cinnamon, allspice, cloves
paste wax
white household glue

Equipment
electric drill and ¼″ bit
soft cloth
compass
string
pencil
electric craft tool (commonly used for egg decorating), if possible, a model with a flexible arm extension
emery cutting wheel to fit craft tool
artist's knife with #11 blade
lightweight cardboard

Drill ¼″ holes in each end of the gourd.

To give the cured and cleaned gourd its brown coloring, preheat a conventional oven to 300° F. With a soft cloth, apply a light coat of cooking oil over the gourd rind. Turn the oven off; then put the gourd inside to toast lightly as the oven cools. Remove the gourd when it is cool enough to handle. Reheat the oven to 300° F.; then turn the oven off and put the gourd back in while the oven cools. You may need to repeat this procedure several times until the gourd obtains an even, bronzed finish.

Following the instructions and the motif in Transferring and Marking Designs (page 108), mark the equator of the gourd with a compass. With string, divide the gourd into two equal segments and mark on the equator line. Adjust the compass arm so that the diameter will be slightly smaller than one of these segments. With the point of the compass at one mark on the equator line, draw a circle. Repeat from the mark on the other side of the equator.

Using the diagram of the eight-pointed star on page 109 as a pattern, with the pencil, draw a star within each circle. (Exact measurements are not possible since the size and shape of your gourd will vary.) Turn the pattern for the eight-pointed star on a diagonal and draw a second star pattern overlaying the first in each circle.

Using the electric tool and emery cutting wheel, trace along all pattern lines to etch the pattern lightly into the surface.

With an artist's knife, cut through the shaded areas of the pattern in the gourd and remove scrap pieces. Cut a ½″-square plug in the bottom of the gourd and reserve the plug.

Finish by applying paste wax with a soft cloth.

Make a tassel and assemble the pomander as described for the Light Brown Pierced Pomander (page 113).

Green Carved Ornament

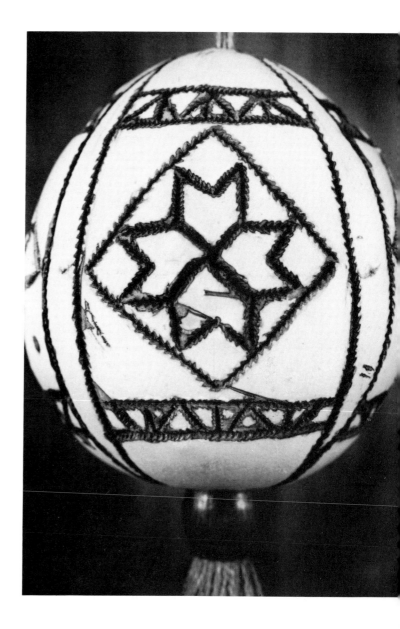

Materials
ornamental gourd, freshly picked
water-base leather dye
wooden bead
2 skeins embroidery floss
white household glue

Equipment
compass
string
pencil
linoleum-cutting tool with V-shaped gouge
soft cloth
hand or electric drill with a small bit
microwave oven
silica gel
sand
casserole
artist's knife with #11 blade
lightweight cardboard

Following the instructions and the motif in Transferring and Marking Designs (page 108), mark the equator of the gourd with a compass. With a string, divide the gourd into four equal segments and mark these on the equator line. Adjust the arm of the compass so that the diameter will be slightly larger than two segments; then with the point of the compass at each of the marks, draw four circles.

Using a linoleum-cutting tool with a V-shaped gouge, incise the diamond shape that surrounds the stars. Tape the hand holding the gourd. Work with a rocking motion, pressing down rather than forward. Freshly cut areas of a gourd will absorb the dye more readily than cuts that have dried for a few hours. To take advantage of the different coloring effects, allow these first cuts to dry for 3 or more hours.

With the same tool, carve the remaining pattern.

Stain immediately with full strength water-base leather dye. (The dye will be darker in freshly carved areas.) Wipe off excess dye right away with a cloth and allow to dry completely.

Drill ¼" vent holes at each end of the gourd. Following the instructions in Microwave Curing (page 107), slowly process the gourd in the microwave oven. Be sure to observe the precautions: unobstructed vent holes; water in the oven with the gourd; 2-minute cycles; and letting the gourd cool inside the oven.

With the artist's knife, cut a ½"-square plug in the bottom of the gourd as described in the microwave drying instructions and complete the drying in silica gel.

Make a tassel and assemble the ornament as described for the Light Brown Pierced Pomander (page 113), omitting the spices.

Clove-Studded Pomander

Materials
ornamental gourd, freshly picked
water-base leather dye
whole cloves
wooden bead
2 skeins embroidery floss
white household glue

Equipment
compass
string
pencil
artist's knife with #11 blade
star-shaped leather stamp
hammer
soft cloth
awl
hand or electric drill
microwave oven
silica gel
sand
casserole
lightweight cardboard

Following the instructions and the motif in Transferring and Marking Designs (page 108), mark the equator on the gourd with a compass. With a string, divide the gourd into four segments and mark these segments on the equator. Adjust the compass arm so that the diameter will be slightly less than two segments (or one-half the gourd). With the point at each of the marks, draw four circles.

With the artist's knife, incise all lines of the pattern. To make the stars as shown in the photograph, place a leather stamp on the gourd and tap firmly with a hammer.

Dye the gourd with a water-base leather dye; then quickly remove excess dye with a soft cloth. Allow to dry completely.

Using a circular motion of the awl, make small holes in the gourd. Push the cloves into these holes.

Drill ¼″ ventilation holes in each end of the gourd and process in the microwave oven following instructions for Microwave Curing (page 107). With the artist's knife, cut a ½″-square plug from the end as described in the microwave drying instructions and complete the drying in silica gel.

Make a tassel and assemble the pomander as described for the Light Brown Pierced Pomander (page 113), omitting the spices.

Waxed-Lined Gourd Bowl

Materials
calabash gourd, cured and cleaned
solvent-base leather dye or wood stain
polyurethane finish
paraffin

Equipment
flower pot	string
pencil	tape measure
hand or electric saw	graphite paper
vise	electric craft tool with
wood rasp	router bits and emery
spoon	cutting wheel
2 brushes	tin can
soft cloth	cooking pan
tracing paper	paintbrush

Be sure that the outer skin of the gourd is completely scraped away. Invert a flower pot of appropriate size over the top of the gourd so that the lip of the pot is parallel to the tabletop. With a pencil, mark a line around the gourd, following the lip of the pot.

With a hand saw (or an electric saw with the gourd in a vise), cut along the penciled line and remove the top of the gourd. With the wood rasp, smooth the lip of the gourd bowl.

Darken the rind of the gourd with leather dye or wood stain applied with a brush. Allow to set (the time will vary, depending on how dark you wish your gourd bowl to be). Remove excess dye with a soft cloth. As soon as the gourd is dry, apply a protective polyurethane finish.

Designs from Indian pottery are well-suited to this gourd bowl as illustrated by the bowl in the photograph, the pattern for which is given below. Choose a pattern from a pottery book as your inspiration and draw or trace the pattern onto tracing paper.

Tie a string around the gourd about one-third of the way down from the open lip and parallel to the lip; your design should be applied above this line for the most satisfying proportions. With a tape measure,

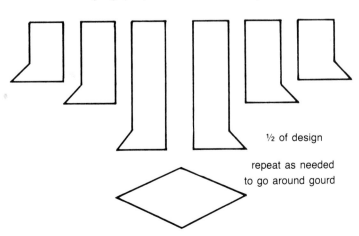

½ of design

repeat as needed
to go around gourd

determine the length of this line around the gourd and divide it by the width of the pattern you have chosen. In this way you can determine how many pattern repeats will fit onto the bowl; adjust the space between the repeats to make your pattern work out evenly.

On the string, mark off the calculated number of repeats to make sure you have figured correctly. With graphite paper, transfer your design from the tracing paper to the gourd, fitting the pattern within each marked repeat space.

With the electric craft tool and a small router bit, outline each element of the design. Then, with a larger router bit, scrape the areas between the lines just deep enough to barely scratch the pith below the tough rind.

Use the cutting disk to smooth the edges and clean the corners of the design. Erase any remaining graphite or pencil marks.

Melt the paraffin in a tin can that has been set in a pan of water in a make-shift double boiler. For safety, closely follow the instructions on the package of paraffin. Brush the liquid paraffin evenly over the interior of the bowl to waterproof it.

Gourd Drum

Materials
calabash gourd with prominent neck, cured and
  cleaned
rawhide
4 pairs leather shoelaces
wooden macrame ring
wooden beads
2 seashells
wood/leather glue

Equipment

pencil	revolving hole punch
books	eraser
hand or electric drill	craft knife with basic
hand or electric saw	pointed blade
vise	push pins
scissors	awl

Note: The diameter of the macrame ring, length of
the shoelaces, number of beads, and the amount of
rawhide needed for the drum head will vary with the
size of the gourd.

Changes in humidity may cause the drum head to
stretch. To allow for adjustments, make certain that
the holes in the wooden beads are large enough to
allow the spliced laces to pass through easily.

PREPARING THE GOURD AND RAWHIDE
Indicate the level at which the base will be removed from the body of the gourd by marking with a
pencil. Stack books to the level of the pencil mark,
place the pencil on top of the stack of books, and
align the pencil with the mark on the gourd. (Diagram
1.) Hold the pencil in place while rotating the gourd
against the pencil to mark a cutting line.

Drill a hole on the penciled line. Insert the saw
blade and cut along the line to separate the base
from the body of the gourd. (If you are using an
electric saw, first secure the gourd in a vise.) Remove inner skin. Drill a small vent hole in the neck.

Place the gourd (cut edge down) on the piece of
rawhide, avoiding thin or weak areas in the hide.
Trace around the gourd with a pencil, marking a
circle on the hide. Draw a concentric circle with a
radius 1½″ larger than the first. Using scissors, cut
along the line marked for the larger circle.

To mark the circle for punching, fold the circle of
hide in half and then in quarters, creasing the fold
lines at the cut edge. Unfold and mark each crease
with a pencil dot 1″ inside the cut edge. Between
each pair of adjacent dots, mark two more dots,
spacing the dots evenly for a total of twelve dots
around the circle of rawhide. The dots should be no
closer than 1½″.

Note: The number of holes and the spaces between them will vary according to the size of your
gourd; adjust accordingly.

Make small holes in the rawhide at the penciled dots, using a hole punch. Erase all pencil marks.

ASSEMBLING THE DRUM

Soak the drum head in water for 30 minutes or more until the rawhide is soft and pliable.

With the craft knife, join one pair of leather shoelaces by splicing. (Diagram 2.) Make a slit in pieces 1 and 2 slightly longer than the width of the lace. Thread point A on piece 2 through slit B on piece 1 and then through slit C on piece 2. Pull the loop closed, as shown. Wrap a third lace around one side of the macrame ring twelve times and loosely tie the free ends of the laces together to secure temporarily.

Note: This temporary wrapping will serve as spacer, separating the ring from the neck of the gourd. As permanent knots are tied with the spliced laces, the temporary wrapping can then be removed, providing spaces to insert permanent lacing.

To assemble the drum, place the gourd in the center of the rawhide circle. Place the ring with the temporary wrapping over the neck of the gourd. On the same side of the gourd as the temporary wrapping, secure the rawhide to the gourd at a point 1″ above the cut edge of the gourd by inserting a push pin through one punched hole in the rawhide and into the gourd. Repeat through two adjacent holes to secure the rawhide. Rotate the gourd 90 degrees so that the push pins and wrapping are on the back side of the gourd as work begins.

Note: Rawhide is soft and pliable and relatively weak when wet; avoid abrupt movements and excessive tension while lacing.

Thread a bead onto the spliced lacing. Slip the lacing over the ring and down between the ring and the neck of the gourd; then pull the splice into position between the ring and neck to conceal it. Tie a lark's head knot with lacing, positioning the bead on the lacing so that it is held between the right and left loops of the knot. (Diagram 3.) When additional splices are made, conceal each splice beneath the ring as before.

Insert one end of the lacing through the nearest punched hole in the rawhide. Pull this lace down to remove slack between the ring and the drum head; then pull up. Loop the lace over and behind the ring, and pull down again to remove the slack. Tie a second lark's head knot.

Continue lacing to join the ring to the drum head, tying a lark's head knot on the ring to secure each joining. Remove the temporaray wrapping on the ring as working space is needed, and use an awl to force the lace through as space diminishes between the ring and the gourd.

When all holes in the rawhide drum head have been used and eleven knots have been tied to the ring, secure the remaining ends of the lacing to the ring with an overhand knot. Trim lacing to leave ends about 8″ long.

Drill holes in the seashells according to the instruc-

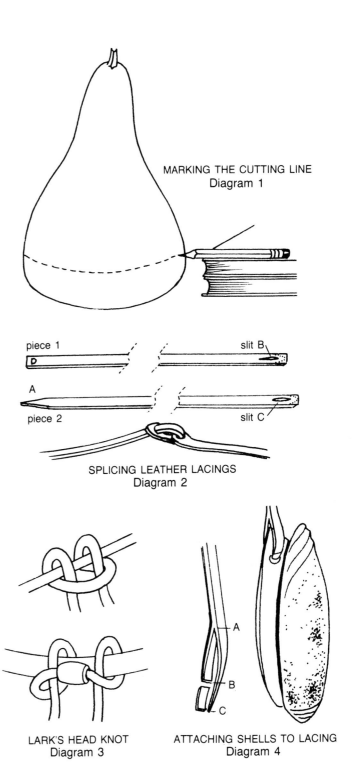

MARKING THE CUTTING LINE
Diagram 1

piece 1   slit B

A

piece 2   slit C

SPLICING LEATHER LACINGS
Diagram 2

LARK'S HEAD KNOT
Diagram 3

ATTACHING SHELLS TO LACING
Diagram 4

tions in Drilling Shells (page 26). Attach shells to the ends of the leather lacings by slitting the lace lengthwise to A. (Diagram 4.) Taper one half to B, as shown, and cut opposite half at C. Thread B through the hole in the shell and tuck into slit A. Glue C over B with wood/leather glue. (See Suppliers, page 150.)

Note: The leather will shrink slightly as it dries, making the drum taut. Twenty-four hours or more may be required for complete drying of the drum head.

FEATHERS: Nature's Palette

Feathers have been a fascination for man since he first picked one from the ground and put it in his hair. From a single feather as ornament it was not far to feathers combined in ceremonial robes and majestic ritual dress. Primitive cultures admired feathers not only for their iridescent beauty, but also as a mystical symbol of the spirit, which could float away from earth and the human body.

The American Indians used feathers to distinguish rank in the tribe and to honor noble deeds in battle.

Today, from prima ballerinas to rock stars, the imagery of feathers is still important to performers. The age-old enchantment of feathers will be apparent to you as well, as you begin to put them into your own designs. The colors are those of precious jewels, the tactile quality sensuous and yielding. And perhaps nowhere else is the harmony of nature more evident than in the colors and patterns combined in feather pelts.

FINDING FEATHERS

To have on hand a workable number and variety of feathers, you must generally mail-order feather pelts. (See Suppliers, page 150.) A skin of the English ring-neck pheasant, which is common in the northern United States, is a good choice for a beginning designer; it has a workable variety of color, texture, and sizes in one skin and is reasonably priced. Other pheasant skins available through the mail are the Golden, Lady Amherst, Reeves, and Silver pheasants, which range in price from $5 to $25 per pelt. Goose, turkey, chicken, and duck feathers are often strung together and sold by the foot; they are also priced by the ounce.

Feathers from local fowls and wild birds can be a helpful and inexpensive supplement to mail-order supplies. Where wild birds are concerned, you, as a craftsperson, are regulated by the same seasonal and bag limit restrictions as a hunter. If you have friends who hunt pheasant, grouse, and duck, and who are willing to save the skins for you, you can easily dry the skins yourself. Scrape a fresh skin well and sprinkle a heavy layer of salt or borax over the skin. Leave the skin to cure in a dry spot for about one week.

You may not legally clean any skin outside of the state and federal hunting seasons, not even those birds killed on the road. And only tribal American Indians are permitted to have eagle feathers in their possession.

Domesticated fowls are another local source for feathers, some in exciting patterns and colors. Visit the poultry exhibition at the country fair to locate the breeders in your area.

Sporting goods stores and catalogs often stock small amounts of feathers for those who tie their own fishing flies. And if there is still an old-fashioned millinery house nearby, they are certain to have exotic feathers.

DESIGNING WITH FEATHERS

The most elegant feather jewelry is that which has a definite, structured design, rather than a random arrangement. The projects shown here are excellent examples of strong designs where color, pattern, and texture are important considerations.

Color

Begin with color combinations that are familiar to you—blue and rust, gold and brown, black and white, green and blue—then experiment to find more personalized combinations. The strong patterns and iridescence of feathers make possible unusual designs even when using "safe," neutral tones such as brown, gray, and beige. Color combinations that you might not risk in other materials, such as dark green and red orange, will blend easily and dramatically with feathers when set off by white. Take hints from the brilliant combinations that occur naturally.

Pattern

Pattern works in a feather design at two levels. First, the individual feather often has a distinct pattern, and second, the way in which feathers are used together creates an overall pattern. Successful designs are achieved if you arrange feathers so that the patterns complement each other.

For instance, the blue, hairy feathers from the tail of an English ring-neck pheasant will create a smooth, solid area in your design if they are used alone. However, the same feather can create a tweed effect when alternated with blue almond feathers from the back of the same pelt.

By using the black and white striped feathers from the silver pheasant, you can achieve a classic herringbone pattern. The dark scalloped edge on the gold feathers of the Reeves pheasant forms a distinctive outline for the earrings shown on page 123.

Texture

In the hatband shown on page 123, a band of smooth, patterned feathers is contrasted with a center rosette of full, fluffy feathers in a clear example of using texture to enhance a design. The pattern of an individual feather contributes to visual texture, but additional textural interest can be created in the way feathers are trimmed and glued. On the flat band, the patterned feathers were trimmed at the ends so the layers would lie flat; the fluffy, irregular ends of the center feathers were left as is so they would stand out for more fullness.

The amount of glue applied can also affect the texture. For a flat layer of feathers, pick up a small amount of glue on the plucked tip of the feather and press the feather in place. With more glue on the feather and by positioning the feather without pressing, you

can create a raised effect. After glueing, if you press the plucked end of the feather down, you can raise the fluffy end.

GLUEING FEATHERS

A heavy-bond craft glue is well suited to feathers because the thick glue can be put down in very small amounts and will not run or slide. For surfaces as small as the earrings, however, it is easier to use an acetone-base glue, which bonds well in pin-head amounts and dries quickly.

Feathers have a natural oil coating that is water repellent. It can be very frustrating when the glue responds "like water off a duck's back." Thus, feather-to-feather bonding is more difficult than glueing feathers to a felt or suede backing. Although it is not always possible with something as small as earrings, try to leave some surface of the backing open until the last few feathers.

Feathers are more durable than they appear; if crushed or separated in handling, they can be lightly steamed to regain their original shape.

do not need to lie perfectly flat to adhere well when using heavy-bond white glue.

Cut suede into a strip ½″ × 10½″. Cut soutache into two 1½″-long pieces. Punch a hole in each end of the suede strip with the leather punch. String soutache through each hole for the necklace ties and knot both ends of the soutache to keep it from slipping out of the holes. Trim the loose ends close to the knots to prevent fraying.

With a permanent marking pen, draw a circle the size of a large pea in the center of the suede strip.

Trim two or three long feathers to 2″ lengths. Position the feathers so that the pretty ends are facing away from the center of the choker. Glue feathers to one side of the choker just outside the center mark, overlapping the feathers. Repeat with two or three feathers on the opposite side of the center mark.

Cut more feathers in 1″ lengths and glue to the center, positioning the blunt tips inside the center mark to form a complete circle. With each feather, overlap half of the adjacent feathers, but leave a small area of suede visible inside the center mark; you'll need some suede surface to glue the next layer of feathers.

Trim feathers for the center to ½″ and neatly glue them in a tight circle, being careful to cover glue marks from the previous circle of feathers.

As the glue begins to dry, press the tip of the scissors into the center of the rosette of feathers. In this way you will lift the feathery outside ends for a fuller, fluffier effect.

When the glue is completely dry, with a toothpick place a very small dot of white glue in the center of the rosette. Place seed beads or a small shell over the glue to finish the choker.

Feather Chokers

Materials
soft brown suede
brown soutache braid
feathers
heavy-bond white craft glue
seed beads or small shell

Equipment
scissors
leather hole punch
permanent marking pen
toothpicks

Hints on Glueing: Place a small amount of glue on a pad. Pick up a small dot of glue on the underside of each feather and press it gently into place. Feathers

Feather Earrings

Materials
suede
feathers
acetone-base glue
double-pronged bale findings
14K gold or gold-filled earring hoops

Equipment
scissors
small needle-nose pliers
thick sewing needle

Hints on Glueing: Acetone-base glue is very fast drying. Therefore, place only three or four drops on a suede pad at one time. Pick up a small amount of glue on each feather and press the glued end to the suede to bond tightly.

Cut two teardrop shapes out of suede, each 1¼" long.

Glue seven to nine background feathers to the suede shapes following the teardrop shape and placing the feathers so that they extend beyond the suede about ¼". The feathers should overlap each other thickly to form a solid background. Remember that you are making a pair of earrings that should match as closely as possible. Choose feathers that match each other in size and color and work on both earrings at the same time.

Form a strong central design by using feathers with a distinctive pattern or edging. Use enough feathers to cover all the suede and the glued ends of the background feathers.

The smallest feathers (neck feathers about ¼" long) should be at the top of the teardrop. Glue these carefully so as little glue as possible shows. This is one place where you will find it difficult not to glue feather to feather. Test the feather after the glue has dried to make sure it has bonded well.

When the glue is dry, turn the suede over and cover the entire back with the same type of feathers that you used for the background on the front side. Again, be careful to finish neatly and let dry.

With needle-nose pliers, bend one prong of a two-pronged bale flat.

Make a hole in the top of the teardrop with a sewing needle. Place the unbent prong through the hole and pinch the bale tightly closed with the pliers. The bale should cover the raw edge of glue. Slide the earring onto a hoop.

Feather Hatband

Materials	Equipment
felt	tweezers
nylon tape fastener	paintbrush for contact
contact cement	cement
6 ring-neck	scissors
pheasant hides	
turquoise cabochon (optional)	

Cut a strip of felt 1½" wide and of a length equal to the circumference of the crown of your hat plus 1" for overlap.

Cut two pieces of nylon tape fastener, each 1½" long. Glue one piece of fastener to the top on one end of the felt strip. Glue the second piece to the underside of the opposite end of the felt strip; allow to dry.

Lay the band on a work table and apply a thin layer of contact cement to one side of the felt band, being careful not to get it on the nylon tape fastener.

While this is drying, choose feathers and pluck them from the skin. Trim close to the patterned area around each feather and place these colorful, oval ends in rows to enable you to match feathers on each side of the hatband for a more uniform appearance.

Apply a second layer of glue to each end of the hatband in 3" sections at a time. Let dry until tacky.

Apply feathers one at a time to the band, overlapping each feather so that the felt is completely concealed.

Keep working from each end until you reach the middle of the felt strip. Using the longest feathers, create a crown effect as shown in the photograph by applying first a feather to one side and then to the other. Apply the center flower design last. Allow to dry. Apply a turquoise cabochon in the center.

Pine Needle Basket

The tradition of coil baskets crosses many cultures and continents, varying significantly only in the materials that are native to the basket maker's home. In a tradition passed down through families for 250 years, the Gullah women near Charleston, South Carolina, coil baskets of sea grasses with pine needles incorporated in dark contrasting bands.

The source of sea grass is rapidly diminishing, however, as the suburban sprawl of Charleston encroaches on the natural habitat of the grass. Pine needles, on the other hand, are fallen materials and are abundantly available to everyone. Instructions are given here for a basket that is made entirely of pine needles and stitched with raffia.

Long pine needles are the easiest to handle. If you live in the South, look for the longleaf, slash, or loblolly pine needles. In the Western states, the ponderosa, digger, and coulter pine needles grow up to 10" long. Basket makers in the Northeast may want to rely on mail-order sources, however, since the pine needles in New England are short and more difficult to coil. (See Suppliers, page 150.)

Materials
6 ounces long pine needles
½ pound raffia
¾" long piece plastic drinking straw, at least ¼" in diameter (optional)
clear varnish (optional)

Equipment
scissors
stock pot
terry cloth towel
crewel embroidery needle (or any blunt tapestry needle
small paintbrush (optional)

Cut the stem ends from the pine needles and drop the needles into a pot of scalding water. Turn the heat off beneath the pot and let the needles soak for 1 hour. Remove the needles from the water, roll them in a towel, and let stand for 3 hours until they are damp and flexible. If you don't finish the basket in 1 day, roll the pine needles in a towel to keep them damp.

Split a length of raffia into two long strips. Thread one strip through the tapestry needle. Bundle twenty-four pine needles together with the uncut, or pointed, ends together. You may wish to use a plastic straw to hold the bundle of pine needles together, or you may simply grasp the bundle firmly with your fingers. Hold the pine needles in your left hand with the pointed ends toward the right.

Secure the raffia to the pine needle bundle, about 2" from the pointed ends by laying one end of the raffia parallel to the bundle of needles and then wrapping the raffia around the bundle and over the end a few times. (Diagram 1.) Use this same procedure each time you must add another length of raffia.

Continue wrapping the raffia around the pine needle bundle for 1½". (Leave about ½" free at the pointed end.)

Curl the pointed ends of the pine needles back to the wrapped bundle and secure them with more wrapping until the ends are concealed. (Diagram 2.) Push the needle from front to back through the center of the loop formed, as shown, and bend the pine needle bundle tightly around the loop to start the coils. (Diagram 3.) Mark the beginning of this second coil with a contrasting thread and begin each new coil at this point to keep the basket perfectly round.

With about ⅛" between stitches, wrap the raffia around the pine needles and back through the center of the first coil until you have completed the second coil. (Diagram 4.)

Add three pine needles, cut end first, and push them as far into the center of the bundle as possible. For the entire project, continue pushing three pine needles into the center of the bundle every few stitches, always keeping the bundle of pine needles the same relative thickness.

At the beginning of the third coil, push the needle from front to back through the outside edge of the second coil, about one-third the width of the coil, and between the stitches of the second coil. (Diagram 5.) This should form a stitch that leans slightly. Now make a stitch through the same spot in the second coil, so that it leans in the opposite direction, forming a V-shaped stitch. Continue around the third coil with V-shaped stitches spaced between the single stitches of the second coil.

For the fourth and all consecutive rows, align the V-shaped stitches with the stitches of the previous row. (Refer to the photograph of the finished basket.)

When you come to the end of a piece of raffia, tie another piece to the end of the preceding length with a square knot and conceal the knot between the coils. Always split the raffia before knotting it onto the other end.

Continue coiling the pine needles and stitching with raffia until you have ten full coils.

Begin the eleventh coil at the mark of the first coil, but *directly on top of the tenth coil.* Simply raise the pine needle bundle to form the sides as you continue stitching. Make an additional fifteen coils, one on top of another, for the sides, for a total of twenty-five coils to finish the basket.

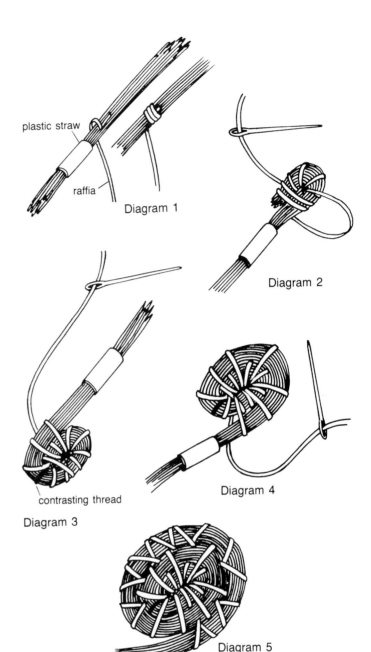

plastic straw
raffia
Diagram 1

Diagram 2

contrasting thread
Diagram 3

Diagram 4

Diagram 5

Use these basic instructions to make a basket of any shape by simply changing the alignment of the coils—sloping gently out, or straight up for a cylinder as shown here, or sloping gently in. Always change direction in a line with the mark of the first coil to assure even roundness.

On the last, or top, coil continue the full thickness until you have stitched past the beginning mark of the first coil. Then stop adding pine needles and continue stitching until all the existing needles are covered. Do not cut the needles off at one point or a blunt end that is hard to conceal will result. Wrap the raffia over the ends of the final needles and knot the raffia. Use the needle to pull the knots back into the pine needles and clip the excess raffia.

Pine needles often darken as they age, creating a mellow contrast with the lighter colored raffia. If desired, brush a thin coat of varnish on the finished basket to preserve the pine needles.

Loblolly Pine

PINE CONES: Spiky Wooden Blossoms

Pine cones are among the most versatile and the most plentiful of natural materials. Their overlapping scales and subtle gray to brown coloring may not need any enhancement at all; two or three individual cones are beautiful at the base of a pottery bowl or live plant. Yet the repetitive pattern of scales can also be dramatized in projects that combine many cones of the same or varying sizes and types—a kind of natural op art effect. The wreaths, basket, and other projects following this section are good examples of how to make the most out of nature's exquisite forms.

GATHERING AND IDENTIFYING

As you work with pine cones, you will discover a tremendous variety of colors, scale formations, and overall shapes. It is a fascinating revelation that while we tend to lump all conifers together, each species produces a distinctive cone as its signature.

You may occasionally want to work with unusual pine cones from other areas of the country, such as a giant cone from the Northwest, but there is a real pleasure and more than a little satisfaction in seeking out the uniqueness of pine cones right where you live. There also is a practical advantage of working with local pine cones, for you can substitute cones from your own area for a similarly shaped cone that may be expensive or unavailable to you.

The short, oval shape is characteristic of the cones of hard pines throughout the United States, making them the best choices for pine cone roses and for wreaths. In contrast, soft pines have what is known as "stalk," or elongated cones. These long cones tend to curve on the tree, making them more suited to designs where they are placed on their sides rather than standing on end.

One of the more unusual of the soft pines is the sugar pine, which produces giant 16" cones that grow only in mountainous regions of California. At the opposite extreme are the piñon pines of western Texas and New Mexico. Piñon cones are 2" to 3" long and have large, edible seeds. Their light golden color and the unique seeds make them an excellent specimen cone.

The spruce varieties that grow in the United States also have elongated, or "pendant," cones, but they are easily distinguished from pines because the scales of spruce cones are soft and thin, overlapping in snug shingles. A

Ponderosa Pine

White Spruce

typical shape centers the wreath on page 131. To get to the seeds, squirrels strip the softer scales of the spruce, leaving a pile of cobs and scales scattered on the forest floor.

If the cones are isolated from the tree, it is often difficult to tell the difference between the cones of a hemlock and those of black and red spruce. The pattern of growth on the tree distinguishes the cones, however. Spruce cones hang down from the branch behind the tip; hemlock are "terminal" cones that grow only at the tip of the branch.

In their natural state, tamarack and larch cones from northeastern United States resemble small roses. Unusual for conifers, these trees are deciduous, losing their needles each fall, but the tenacious cones may stay on the branches for two years.

Another natural rose shape is found on the deodar cedar. The cones grow upright from the branch to a length of 3" to 5", but when they mature in two years, the cones disintegrate, or lose their scales except for the top few inches, which forms a multi-petaled "rose."

The hairy cones of Douglas fir from the Rockies are useful for decoration. But no other fir cone will be recommended for craft projects because the upright cones of true firs disintegrate on the trees, leaving stalks that look very much like old-fashioned Christmas tree candles waiting to be lit.

The photographs of pine cones throughout this section will help you identify the most common cones in your area. Gathering your own cones and learning more about them is another dimension in personalizing a naturecraft.

WORKING WITH PINE CONES

If you have ever made a pine cone wreath, you know the hazards involved—scratched hands as you wedge the pine cones tightly together, and no matter how you push, there are still gaps between some cones. There is a simple remedy for this problem. By simply soaking the cones in water for 10 minutes you can avoid both the scratches and the gaps. As the pine cones soak, they contract. In this stage you can wire them closely together. As the cones dry, they spread until they fit snugly together, making the wreath or other shape much tighter and fuller than you could make with dry cones.

It is important to wrap the cones with wire (as described below) *before* soaking them. Once the scales contract, it will be difficult to insert the wire. Another hint: don't soak the cones longer than 10 minutes, or it can take several days for the cones to dry out and look full on the wreath.

Soaking is most effective when attaching hard cones to a wire form that will not give as the cones spread. It is not recommended for soft cones or cones secured to a surface with glue.

ATTACHING CONES

As a rule, pine cones should be attached to wire forms which can support their weight. They may be wired onto the form or attached with cooking glue. If the cones must cover a broad flat area, such as the heart shown on page 129,

Pitch Pine

Piñon Pine

Norway Spruce "Cob"

Norway Spruce

or if cones of different sizes are used together, it is best to use cooking glue. Cooking glue—a recent introduction to the craft world—is an instant-bond glue that is sold in liquid form. Heat it slowly in a pan on your range and use a toothpick to place a dab of the hot glue onto the form. The liquid glue tends to be stringy when heated, however, and it can be a messy job.

An electric glue gun, which costs from $11 to $15, uses dry sticks of cooking glue. When the gun is plugged in, the stick liquifies, and you "shoot" a dot of glue. One advantage of instant-bond glue is that you do not have to hold the cone in place while the glue dries. The electric glue gun also provides an uncomplicated way to attach nuts and small seed pods to wreaths.

To wire cones onto a vine wreath or wire form, use precut lengths of 18- to 22-gauge florist's wire. About ½″ to 1″ from the stem of the cone, wrap the wire completely around the cone, pushing it between layers of scales to conceal it. Cross the wire ends where they meet and backtrack with each end for a quarter of a circle until the ends are on opposite sides of the cone. (Diagram 1a.) Then pull the wire ends down to the stem end of the cone and twist the wires around each other. (Diagram 1b.)

ATTACHING NUTS TO A PINE CONE WREATH

A wide variety of nuts is available in the grocery stores from Thanksgiving to Christmas—pecans, walnuts, Brazil nuts, almonds, and hazelnuts. Their small size and hard shells make nuts somewhat tedious to secure to a wreath, but they will last as long as the pine cone base if the nuts are debugged first.

Put the nuts in a shallow baking dish along with a baking potato and bake in a 225° F. oven. When the potato is done, any bugs inside the nuts will be dead and future entries discouraged.

The simplest and quickest way

Diagram 1a

Diagram 1b

to secure nuts to a wreath is with an electric glue gun. But old hosiery and florist's wire provide a less expensive, although more time-consuming, alternative.

Cut the hosiery into small squares. With light-colored hosiery over light-colored nuts and dark hosiery over darker nuts, the hosiery squares are almost invisible when they are pulled tightly around the nuts. The corners of the hosiery square provide a "stem"; twist florist's wire around the loose hosiery ends. (Diagram 2.) Then wire the nuts onto the wreath form.

Diagram 2

White Pine

Pine Cone Heart

One successful formula for creativity is to rethink traditional forms and materials. This small pine cone heart shape is designed to grace your walls throughout the winter months—right up through Valentine's Day! The tiny spruce cones are the perfect size and weight for the lightweight plastic foam base.

Materials
8″ square of plastic foam
brown liquid shoe polish
120 cones of white spruce, hemlock, or larch
U-shaped florist's pins

Equipment
pencil
sharp kitchen knife
garden shears
cooking glue or electric glue gun with glue sticks

With a pencil, mark a heart outline on the plastic foam and cut along the outline with a knife. Use the scraps of foam like sandpaper to smooth the cut edges of the heart. Paint the foam with brown liquid shoe polish and allow to dry.

Hemlock or larch cones are well suited to a small heart, but if they are not available, trim the floret end from soft, white spruce cones with garden shears. The small heart shown here was made from the trimmed white spruce cones. Soak the pine cones in water for 10 minutes.

Use a generous dollop of glue to secure each cone to the foam base, starting near the center of the heart and working out to the sides. Let the glue dry overnight; then reglue any loose cones.

From the back of the heart, push a U-shaped florist's pin into the foam to serve as a hanger; the open end of the pin should be pointing up.

Double Bordered Pine Cone Wreaths

Pine cones blend compatibly with dried flowers and herbs in a harvest wreath for fall decoration and with fresh fruit above the mantel at Christmas. In January, fill in between the borders of pine cones with nuts, seedpods, and other cones for a wreath that will warm the family room until spring.

One permanent pine cone wreath base will last for many years and can be easily transformed to reflect the changing seasons. Instructions are given here for two different double-bordered pine cone wreath bases, one completed with milkweed seedpods and the second with squirrel cobs.

Milkweed Seedpod Wreath

Sliced Cone Wreath

Pine cones used as the single material in a wreath —but sliced, angled, and sized for a variety of fascinating textures—present a somewhat formal appearance. This wreath is made from only two varieties of pine cones, but the effect is that of a wreath of many different materials. This is also a good way to make a few pine cones cover a lot of space.

Materials
17 loblolly pine cones
24 small Virginia pine or hemlock cones
½" plywood wreath form (16" in diameter)

Equipment
electric saw
long-nosed pliers
electric glue gun with glue sticks

Begin by using the electric saw to slice off the tip and the bottom of each loblolly cone. Slice the middle section of cone in half lengthwise. Soak all cones in water for 10 minutes.

Using the photograph as a guide, glue cone tips side by side around the entire outside circle of the wreath form. Glue cone bottoms around the outside circle at every other cone tip.

Fill the center of the wreath by glueing cone halves flat onto the plywood base.

Fill the inside circle and spaces between cone bottoms on the outside circle with clusters of Virginia pine or hemlock cones.

Materials
about 2 dozen large acorns
6 to 8 dozen cones from white pines
wire wreath form (16″ in diameter)
about 18 milkweed seedpods
white household glue
3 to 5 cones of deodar cedar

Equipment
baking pan

Bake the acorns in a 250° F. oven for one hour to kill any insects and discourage future infestations.

Soak the pine cones in water for 10 minutes. Then, wedge them between the wires on the outside edge of the wire wreath form with the tips facing out. Then, wedge pine cones closely together on the inside edge of the form with the tips facing toward the center.

Separate the milkweed seedpod halves and remove all the seeds. Glue the pods, open side up, to the wreath form between the pine cone borders as shown in the photograph. Stagger the pods so that the space between the pine cone borders is completely filled and the wire form is concealed except for a few inches at the bottom.

Glue the deodar cedar cones, which resemble flowers, in a group at the bottom of the wreath. Glue an acorn without a cap in the center of each pod.

Squirrel Cob Wreath

Squirrels clean away the soft scales of spruce cones, leaving reddish "cobs," which are very effective in a wreath, not only because of their color, but also because of the distinctive texture and shape they add to the background pine cones.

Materials
6 to 8 dozen cones from white pine
wire wreath form (16″ in diameter)
about 1 dozen cones from Norway spruce
about 3 dozen cobs from Norway spruce
white household glue
yucca stalk with about 2 dozen blades

Equipment
scissors

Make a double border with the white pine cones as described for the Milkweed Seedpod Wreath.

Arrange the full spruce cones lengthwise between the borders of white pine cones as shown in the photograph and glue in place.

Glue the spruce cobs on either side of the full spruce cones so that the cobs fill in any gaps and conceal the wire form.

Starting at the bottom of the yucca stalk, carefully pull away the long blades. Where each blade grips the stalk there is a concave half-circle, which will add a contrasting light color and unusual shape to the wreath. Cut the blades, leaving about 2″ on the fleshy, stalk end; discard the tip end.

Poke the yucca stems into the cones, spacing them randomly around the wreath; they will dry naturally in the wreath.

Pine Cone Basket

Materials
2 to 3 dozen pine cones in graduated sizes
wire basket form with handle (See Suppliers, page 150.)
pecan or small cone such as red spruce

Equipment
cooking glue or electric glue gun with glue sticks

Soak all pine cones in water for 10 minutes.

With the basket form upside down, shape a flat bottom by wedging a circle of small cones into the top of the dome. These first cones should be inserted so that the stem ends, which are flat, are on the outside of the basket. Try to arrange the cones evenly so that the basket will sit level. Use glue to cement the cones to the basket form.

With the bottom cones in place, turn the basket right side up and fill in a circle of small cones just above the base; these cones should be positioned with the stem ends to the inside. Secure the cones in place with glue.

Fill in another circle of pine cones and glue, working toward the top of the basket and using gradually larger cones as the spaces between the wire form are farther apart near the top. The pine cones in each layer should be approximately the same size so that the top row, or circle, will be even and will conceal the top wire of the basket.

Select enough cones to cover the handle; then soak these cones for about 10 minutes so you can wedge them between the narrow wires of the handle. With soaking, these cones may not need glue.

On the inside of the finished basket, the bottom may have a small gap in the center; fill with a nut or small pine cone.

Pine Cone Roses

In their natural form, tamarack pine, deodar cedar, and the tops of red spruce cones resemble roses. If you cannot find these cones nearby, however, you can cut the base from a fairly large, "round" cone, such as a pitch pine, and then trim it to resemble a rose, as shown in the photograph above. Or, by following the directions below, you can "build" a rose from a cone with hard scales, such as the loblolly and ponderosa pines.

Materials
1 pine cone with hard scales
florist's pick without wire

Equipment
long-nose pliers
cooking glue or electric glue gun with glue sticks

Starting at the stem end of the large cone, pull the individual scales off with the long-nose pliers.

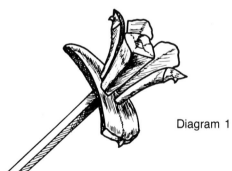

Diagram 1

The florist's pick will serve as a stem. Glue one large scale, lying flat, onto the blunt end of the pick to serve as a base for the "petals" of the rose. In the center of the flat base scale, glue several small scales in an upright circle. (Diagram 1.)

Glue additional layers of "petals," using increasingly larger scales as you work to the outside of the rose form. Once the flat base scale is covered, glue each layer of scales onto the preceding layer.

HOLIDAY GREENERY: Decorating with Native Materials

In Colonial America, homesick pioneer families searched for the holly and boxwood that meant Christmas in England, and they ingeniously adapted what they could find in their new home. Many of their substitutions—cranberries, for example—have become treasured traditions for American generations that have followed.

Their lesson of using what was at hand has practical advantages

today: native materials not only cost less, but will also last longer than purchased greenery, which has often been cut for at least a week when it was purchased. Materials that you gather from your neighborhood make it possible to create original, personalized decorations with the charm and warmth of a traditional Christmas. Even city dwellers may be able to gather native greenery from nearby state parks. You must get permission ahead of time, but often, park officials will direct you to stands of pine and juniper where you may clip branches and pick up pine cones.

CUTTING GREENS

It is a waste to cut greenery that will not last inside the house, so refer to the list on page 137 for the most lasting choices for holiday greens. Keep in mind, too, that careless pruning can ruin the shape of a tree and may kill a shrub. As a general rule, cut just above a new bud so that spring growth will fill in where you took away. A random cut often leaves an exposed stub susceptible to "winter kill," which can go all the way back to the trunk, destroying the whole branch.

There are plants that call for even more careful pruning and some that call for less. Yew, boxwood, and Japanese holly need judicious cutting in winter weather. Even though these plants may be liberally cut during the summer in a close-trimmed hedge, you should take only short clippings in winter. If you cut more than a few inches, you expose tender growth that is used to protection from sun and wind.

Two years' growth can be safely taken from rhododendron, mountain laurel, and andromeda. Count two joints back from the tip of a branch and cut just *above* the second joint. If you cut behind the second joint, the third year wood will not put out new growth in the spring, and there will be an unsightly hole in the shrub.

At the opposite extreme, pine, juniper, and arborvitae are not

weakened by winter cuttings. You can cut the entire branch back to the trunk, but avoid taking too many cuts on one side or you will have a permanently lopsided shape.

CONDITIONING GREENS

The key to making native greens last inside your house is the conditioning you give them before you bring them indoors. Leave the greens in a bucket of water overnight in the garage or cool basement. They need this transitional period to absorb as much water as possible and to adjust to the change in temperature. You can facilitate the water absorption by crushing the stem ends with a hammer or by splitting the ends with several 2"-long vertical cuts.

After conditioning overnight, holly, pine, and cedar stem ends should be dipped in candle wax to seal the resin. Even with this precaution, pine and cedar are not recommended for garlands because they can stain the walls.

The Victorians used ivy abundantly, twined around candlesticks, chandeliers, and stair railings. Out of water, ivy will dry within a week, but if you dip the ivy (stem, leaves, and all) into clear, liquid floor wax and let it dry overnight on newspaper, you can make the ivy appear lush for

much longer. The wax gives ivy such a glossy finish that it appears to be fresh for several weeks.

Magnolia cuttings that are glycerin-cured in the fall will have a lustrous bronze tone that is very appealing at Christmas. If you prefer green magnolia, however, you must cut new branches in December. Stand the branches for 2 days in 1 part glycerin to 2 parts water; then hang the branches upside down in a dark closet for 4 days to keep them green.

Another way to prolong the freshness of greenery is to make wreaths on a sphagnum moss base so that the greenery stems rest in moisture. Instructions for a Sphagnum Moss Wreath Base appear on page 142.

The number of greens practical for decoration increases considerably if you can provide them with a continuous source of water. On the mantel, use any shallow, waterproof container and conceal it with overhanging greenery. Florist's foam is a good base for arrangements of greenery because it not only holds the water supply, but it also acts as support for the stems.

Another hint to having your decorations last: when you "deck the halls," turn the thermostat down!

WORKING WITH GREENERY

After conditioning, cut the branches of greenery into workable-size sprigs. With florist's wire, wrap several sprigs together into small bunches. (Diagram 1.)

Wreaths: Always attach greens so that each sprig or branch lies in the same direction as it circles the wreath. For instance, start at the bottom of a wreath form and work clockwise so that each new bunch of greenery hides the stems of the previously attached greenery. (Diagram 2.)

Greenery must be wired to a sphagnum moss wreath base or to a rigid wire base. But use U-shaped florist's pushpins to secure bunches of greenery to a plastic-wrapped straw wreath form.

Garlands: Boxwood and pittosporum are the best choices for garlands, although pine can be used on a stair railing where it is not resting against a wall. Again, the greenery should be tied into small, workable bunches and aligned in one direction.

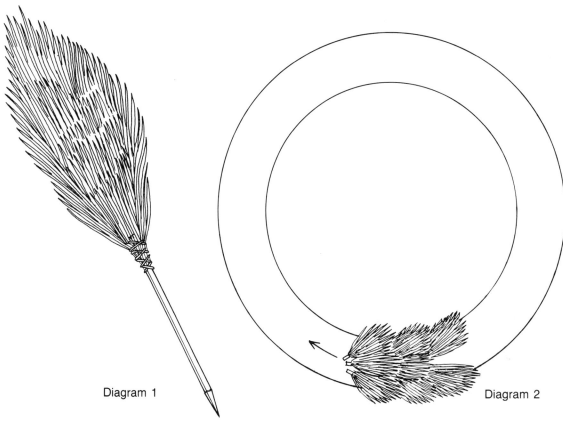

Diagram 1

Diagram 2

Boxwood and pittosporum require a rope support about ¼" thick. If the rope is dyed green, it will take less greenery to conceal it. Tie the bunches of greenery onto the rope with florist's wire.

For a thicker pine garland without using rope, tie each bunch directly on to the preceding bunch. In this method, you are forced to tie the bunches of greenery close together, making a thick garland without gaps.

To hang fruit or ribbon bows on a garland of greenery, put a florist's pick into the fruit (as described below) or bow and wrap the fine wire at the opposite end of the pick around the nails that support the garland.

FRUIT AND BERRIES

Apples, pomegranates, and cranberries take on a wonderful holiday gloss from liquid floor wax, although it should be made clear to guests and family that the apples that look so inviting cannot be eaten. Vegetable oil is an edible gloss, but should be used only where the oil will not get on clothes, linens, or upholstery.

Weight is the most important consideration when decorating with fruit, for it must be securely attached to wreaths and garlands. Use both florist's wire and florist's picks to stabilize fruit.

Push a piece of florist's wire crosswise through the center of the fruit and bring the ends down toward the base of the fruit. If you are *not* attaching a florist's pick, twist these ends together (Diagram 3) and wrap them around a wire wreath base.

To secure fruit on a garland, straw wreath base, or fruit pyramid with a soft base, you must also use a florist's pick. Make a hole in the stem end of the fruit with the sharp end of the pick; then reverse the pick and push the blunt end into the fruit. Twist the ends of the cross wire tightly around the pick. (Diagram 4.)

Many people have been justifiably afraid to experiment with berries other than American holly because of the possible damage to

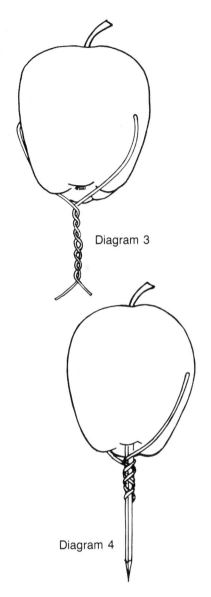

Diagram 3

Diagram 4

rugs and carpeting if berries drop in the house. The plump clusters of nandina, pyracantha, and burford holly can be safely used, however, if they are dipped in clear liquid floor wax, which helps to hold the berries on the stems. Dip clusters of berries and allow to dry overnight on newspaper. (You can reuse the wax many times.) The stems of berry clusters can be wired to florist's picks for more flexibility in arranging.

Rosehips, crab apples, sumac, and magnolia seed pods are also excellent possibilities for color that you may not have considered. Spray the sumac and magnolia pods with inexpensive hair spray to keep the seeds intact.

DECORATING FOR THE HOLIDAYS

For Garlands and Wreaths:

Two or three weeks with conditioning
- Arborvitae
- Boxwood
- Ivy

Ten days with conditioning
- Pine
- Pittosporum
- Juniper
- Eastern Redcedar
- Magnolia
- Holly

For Mantel and Tabletop:

One week in water
- Yew
- Andromeda
- Mountain Laurel
- Rhododendron
- Leucothoe
- Pachysandra
- Elaeagnus
- Acuba (variegated and green)
- Anise
- Cotoneaster
- Mahonia
- Cleyera
- Horsetails
- Cork Elm
- Aspidistra
- Huckleberry branch
- Smilax
- Osmanthus
- Tea Olive

Berries and Seedpods

- Nandina
- Holly
- Pyracantha
- Winterberries
- Rosehips
- Crab Apples
- Sumac
- Magnolia seedpods

Terrarium Tree Ornaments

Materials
silver Christmas tree balls
chlorine bleach
potting soil
princess pine or other lacy evergreen
partridge berry

Equipment
muffin tin
Q-tips®
note paper
knitting needle

Remove the caps from the silver ball ornaments. (Other colored Christmas balls will also work, but they have silver inside and an additional coating outside, so they take twice as long to clean.) Carefully fill each ball with chlorine bleach and set aside for at least 30 minutes to loosen the silver coating. Set the balls upright in a muffin tin to prevent spills. Use a Q-tip® to scrape silver from the inside of the ball; then rinse each ball well to remove all traces of silver. Let the now-clear balls dry for a day or two before filling them.

Make a tiny funnel with note paper and sift loose potting soil into the ball to a depth of ½" to 1".

Princess pine is an evergreen that grows as a runner on the ground and thus has small, shallow roots that are suitable for the Christmas terrarium. With a knitting needle, gently press the pine roots into the potting soil. (You can use any lacy evergreen sprigs, but they will not root and live beyond Christmas.)

Water the potting soil lightly, drop in a few berries for color, and replace the cap. With monthly watering, the terrarium will thrive in a window for several months.

Lunaria Poinsettias

Materials
lunaria (honesty or money plant)
white household glue
sumac berries
clear filament (fishing line)

Equipment
flat hairclip

Dry and shuck the seeds of the money plant in the fall, but leave the iridescent, white circles on the stalk.

Glue lunaria petals to each other, overlapping them slightly to form a circle. A flat, metal hairclip will help to hold the petals in place while you glue them, one at a time, to form the flower.

For hanging, make a generous loop of clear fishing line. With the ends at the center of the lunaria petals, glue the fishing line to the center and hold in place with the hairclip until the glue dries.

When thoroughly dry, dot more glue in the center of the "flower" and add sumac berries to represent the poinsettia center. Glue additional sumac berries to the other side of the ornament.

Dusty Miller Snowflakes

Materials
dusty miller plants

Equipment
sharp garden shears
florist's vials

Dusty miller, the spiky, blue gray foliage of summer gardens takes on a very different role in December. On the Christmas tree, it becomes a living snowflake.

Cut and inserted into tiny florist's vials full of water, the living ornaments will stay fresh for up to 2 weeks. You must plan ahead to bring the dusty miller inside before the first frost. Save the largest plants so you'll have plenty of snowflakes. A 12"-high plant will yield 5 to 7 snowflakes. They will live until Christmas in a sunny window or in a greenhouse.

Clip the ends of the branches to make snowflakes and put them immediately into the water in the florist's vial. The vials are small and the foliage thirsty, so add water to each vial each day and mist the leaves.

Nestle the snowflakes in the green branches of your Christmas tree or in greenery on your mantel for an unusual, wintry decoration.

Spice Tree Ornaments

Materials
whole allspice
whole cloves
cinnamon sticks
star anise
whole nutmeg
cardamom
dried ginger root
florist's wire (22 gauge, 18" lengths)

Equipment
needle
vise
electric drill with 1/16" drill bit

Soak allspice and cloves in warm water for 12 to 24 hours so that they will be soft enough to push wire through. (You may still need to use a needle and thimble to make a hole for the wire.)

Break the cinnamon sticks into ½" pieces.

Star anise is a striking shape, but it is expensive. To make a hole in star anise and nutmeg, fasten the spices in a vise and drill a hole with an electric drill and a 1/16" drill bit. Because of the expense and more complicated drilling required, plan your ornaments so that these are special accents with the bulk of the ornaments made of cinnamon, allspice, and cloves.

Cardamom and dried ginger root, which are light in color, add valuable highlights to the ornaments, but they, too, are expensive and should be used sparingly.

Mark the center of one 18" length of wire and slip the center spice—a large or distinctive shape—into the exact center. Match the patterns on each side of the center so that the sides of the finished ornament will be symmetrical. Work with the wire straight until you have filled all but 3" or 4" at each end.

Bend the spice-filled wire into a wreath, tree, or bell shape. Twist the ends of the wire tightly around each other and bend them into a hook-shape for hanging.

Kissing Ball

Materials
soft-mesh chicken wire
sphagnum moss or Spanish moss
florist's wire
florist's picks
santolina or boxwood
red ribbon
mistletoe
rose hips
rosemary
thyme

Equipment
work gloves
wire cutters
scissors
shears

Wearing gloves, wrap the chicken wire around the sphagnum or Spanish moss, shaping it into a ball. Use florist's wire where necessary to hold the ends of the chicken wire together.

Soak the ball of moss and allow to drain while you attach sprigs of santolina or boxwood onto florist's picks.

Tie a long piece of ribbon to the wire mesh for hanging; then insert the santolina or boxwood into the ball for a round, dense covering of greenery.

Wrap sprigs of mistletoe, rose hips, rosemary, and thyme onto florist's picks and insert into the kissing ball.

Add a bright red bow to the top and hang the kissing ball where it will get the most use!

To keep the kissing ball fresh, mist it every day. Or once a week, remove the bow and dip the entire ball into water; allow to drain and then rehang.

Sphagnum Moss Base

Prolong the freshness of Christmas decorations by keeping the stems of fresh greenery moist in a base of sphagnum moss. Inside the house, a wreath of natural greenery in moss will last up to a month if watered regularly. Outside in cool temperatures and natural rainfall, live greenery arrangements in a sphagnum moss base will last until Easter.

If you will be using only greenery and a lightweight bow for your wreath, make your own base of chicken wire from the instructions given here. For large greenery wreaths or wreaths with fruit, a commercial wreath form of rigid wire should be included within the chicken wire to support the extra weight.

Materials
36"-wide poultry wire (1" hex)
florist's wire
3 (12" × 12") bags sphagnum sheet moss
large wire wreath form (optional)
heavy green garbage bag (optional)

Equipment
wire cutters
gloves
pliers

For a moss wreath 12" in diameter, cut a strip of poultry wire 8" × 36". (For a wreath 24" in diameter, cut two 8" × 36" strips and wire them together for an 8" × 72" length.)

Bring the ends of the wire strips together, overlapping them about 2". Use florist's wire to secure the ends together, forming a circle. (If you are making a wreath that is 24" or larger, place a wire wreath form upside down over the poultry wire circle.)

Soak the sphagnum sheet moss in water for 5 to 10 minutes and then squeeze the excess water out. Tear the moss into strips and place these strips inside the poultry wire (or wire forms, if used).

With gloves to protect your hands, bring the cut edges of the poultry wire together to form a tube over the damp moss (and wire form). Twist the cut ends with pliers to close the tube.

If the moss wreath is to be used inside, it should be wrapped in plastic before the greenery and fruit are attached. Cut a heavy garbage bag into long strips about 2" to 4" wide and spiral these strips around the wire form to contain the moisture.

Garlands of Cranberries or Sweet Gum Balls

Thread strong, transparent fishing line through a needle. Secure the first cranberry or sweet gum ball with a loop and large knot. Slide the remaining berries and gum balls down without gaps.

Fruit Pyramid

The most documented eighteenth-century fruit pyramids were decorated with apples and a pineapple crown, but it is likely that industrious decorators used any colorful combination of available fruits and berries. The fruit pyramid was one of the most popular decorations in early American Christmases, but before the days of wooden, spiked cones, Colonial women improvised a pyramid base with three cabbages in increasingly smaller sizes. After the holidays, the fruit went into pies and the cabbages into the soup pot.

Pineapples, which were imported from the Caribbean, were a treat, and many housewives found themselves torn between using the pineapple on the pyramid or using it for Christmas dinner. To meet both needs, the top of the pineapple was often sliced off and nestled among the thick greenery of the pyramid, while the fruit went to the kitchen. When the top alone was used on the pyramid, it was appropriately called a "deceit."

Materials
3 cabbage heads in
  graduated sizes
large platter
knitting needle or
  barbeque skewer
boxwood sprigs
lemons
florist's picks
holly sprigs
berry clusters

Equipment
large knife
ice pick

Slice the top and bottom from the largest cabbage so that it will sit level; do the same with the medium-size cabbage and place it on top of the first. Cut the smallest cabbage in half and put one half on top of the stack, flat side down. Have someone else hold the cabbages in place while you push a long knitting needle or skewer down through all three heads.

Place loose sprigs of boxwood in a thick border on the platter at the base of the largest cabbage.

Secure lemons onto florist's picks as shown on page 137. Use an ice pick to make holes in the cabbages first; then push the picks with the lemons into the holes in the cabbages, forming roughly parallel circles around the pyramid.

Starting at the bottom, push boxwood sprigs and holly between the lemons, interspersing with berry clusters as needed. There should be enough greenery and berries so that the greenery is held in place by crowding.

(To secure a pineapple or "deceit" on the top, make four holes in the top cabbage with the ice pick. Push the blunt end of a florist's pick into each of these holes so that the sharp end of each pick points up. Push the pineapple down onto these spikes.)

Spanish Moss Wreath

Spanish moss has the same natural water-absorbing properties as sphagnum moss and will keep live greenery looking fresh for several weeks. But Spanish moss has additional appeal; its pale, blue gray coloring and lacy tendrils make a striking Christmas wreath without the addition of greenery.

Materials
Spanish moss
wire or straw wreath form

Equipment
potato and disposable foil roasting pan
or
Diazinon poison and rubber gloves

One word of caution: Spanish moss is a haven for many tiny insects and must be cured before you can use it. (If you gather Spanish moss on vacation in the South, cure it right away or put it into a well-sealed garbage bag and transport it in the trunk of your car.) You can kill the insects in one of two ways. Put the moss in an aluminum foil baking pan with a potato and bake in a 225° F. oven until the potato is done. Any bugs will be killed by the time the potato is cooked.

An alternative to killing the bugs in your oven is to soak the moss for a few minutes in a solution of water and Diazinon. Use one-half strength and follow the instructions on the package. Wear rubber gloves when working with this chemical. Be sure all parts of the moss are submerged in the solution; then spread the moss out in the sun to dry.

To make a decorative wreath of Spanish moss like the one in the photograph that is decorated with cotton bolls, wrap the vinelike moss around a straw wreath form until the straw is concealed. In this way, less moss is required to make a full wreath.

However, if you are using the moss as a moisture-absorbing base to keep greenery fresh, it should be wrapped in many layers around a wire wreath form.

Advent Wreath of Herbs

Materials	Equipment
sphagnum moss	scissors
wire wreath form	pencil
(10″ in diameter)	
florist's wire	
dinner plate	
fresh herbs	
florist's clay	
4 candles	

Soak the sphagnum moss for about 15 minutes in warm water; then squeeze to remove excess water. With the wire wreath form upside down, pack the moss firmly into the wire form, and wrap florist's wire in spirals about 1" apart to hold the moss in place.

Turn the wreath form right side up on the plate. Make holes in the moss with a pencil to keep from breaking the fragile stems of the herbs.

Cut the herbs into 3"-long sprigs and wrap the stems together with wire. Start by making a border of herbs on the outside edge of the wreath, inserting the herb sprigs so that they all point in the same direction. Then fill a border on the inside edge of the wreath with the herb bunches lying in the opposite direction.

At this stage, put a small clump of florist's clay at four points in the moss to stabilize the candles. (Later on, it will be almost impossible to get the clay in place through the layers of herbs.) Push four candles firmly into the clay.

Now fill in the center space between the borders of herbs, clustering several sprigs together in one spot for fullness.

There are no restrictions on the herbs that may be used; include whatever is available in your greenhouse or window garden. If only a few herbs are on hand, make the borders of any lacy, delicate evergreen and fill the center with herbs.

Since the Advent wreath should last one month, it must be misted every day and watered when the moss feels dry. Keep the wreath in bright, indirect sunlight. If you continue watering and misting the herbs, they will last far beyond Advent Sunday as a living winter centerpiece on your dining table.

Cranberry Wreath

Materials
2 to 3 packages fresh cranberries
clear liquid floor wax (optional)
plastic foam wreath base
green foil
flat platter (same diameter as wreath form)
long straight pins
cedar greenery
florist's wire
ribbon

Dip cranberries into liquid floor wax and allow to dry on newspapers overnight.

Wrap the wreath form with dark green foil and put it on a silver tray or a foil-covered platter. (Cranberries will stain, so the platter is a must.)

Use long straight pins to stick the cranberries onto the plastic foam wreath, placing the cranberries as close together as possible.

Tie cedar sprigs together with florist's wire and wrap the wire around the foam wreath. Attach a ribbon bow with florist's wire.

The cranberries will last about one week. To make a hanging wreath of cranberries, use magnolia leaves as a border, stapling them to the back of the foil-covered wreath form.

Pomander Balls &
Christmas Fragrances

The appetizing smell of spices in the house evokes as much festivity as packages under the tree. The pomander ball is a classic accessory for the entire winter, but there are other ways to bring Christmas fragrances into your house and kitchen. If you didn't plan ahead and make pomander balls just after Thanksgiving, puncture several lemons with cloves (a few cloves per lemon) and layer the lemons in a silver bowl with cinnamon sticks and red berries. The warmth of the house will intensify their spicy aroma. The spicy kitchen wreath of cinnamon and applesauce on the facing page also adds the smell of spices to the Christmas holidays.

Materials
florist's wire (optional)
orange, lemon, or lime
pumpkin pie seasoning (or mix your own with ground cinnamon, cloves, nutmeg, allspice, and grated orange rind)
orrisroot (optional)
whole cloves

Equipment
florist's pick
thimble

With the florist's pick, puncture holes about ¼" apart all over the orange, lemon, or lime.

If you want to hang the pomander ball, push a piece of florist's wire through the fruit; make a loop at one end of the wire and pull the loop back into the fruit.

Orrisroot is often hard to find, but it does help to preserve the scent. If you can find it at a health food store, mix it in equal parts with the ground spices. Roll the fruit in the ground spices.

With a thimble to protect your finger, press a whole clove into each of the punched holes.

Roll the fruit in the spice and orrisroot mixture again and hang it in a cool place for about 3 weeks until the fruit is rock-hard.

Spicy Kitchen Wreath

Nothing brings to mind Christmases past more than the smell of spices in the kitchen. Even if you don't do as much cooking as eighteenth-century housewives, your kitchen can still smell like fruitcake and plum pudding and mulled wine. The spicy smell comes from a hardened mixture of apples and cinnamon, and the heat of the kitchen intensifies the delightful, festive smell.

Materials
1 cup apple pulp or applesauce
1½ cups ground cinnamon or ground mixture of
   cinnamon, allspice, and cloves
florist's wire
bittersweet vines
juniper branches with berries
2 (3'-long) pieces jute string
2 small terra cotta pots

To make your own apple pulp, cook apples until they are mushy and put them through a sieve to remove seeds, core, and skin; you may use canned applesauce instead. For each cup of apple pulp, add 1½ cups of spices. Roll the thick mixture (about the consistency of commercial play dough) into small balls.

Stick florist's wire through each ball and make a hook on the far end of the wire; then gently pull the wire hook back into the ball. The ball will dry and harden in 3 to 4 days.

Clip all branches from the bittersweet vines and wrap them into a small (10"-diameter) wreath shape, tucking loose ends inside as you wind the wreath. (See page 74 for instructions on making vine wreaths.)

With florist's wire, attach the juniper sprigs and dough balls at intervals around the wreath.

Slide one piece of jute string through the hole in the bottom of each terra cotta pot and tie a knot larger than the hole. Or attach a small stick to keep the pot from slipping off the jute. With the clay pots thus secured for hanging, tie the jute strings in a bow around the top of the wreath. Add a wire hanger to support the wreath and breathe deeply of spicy Christmas aromas.

Designers & Contributors

The authors would like to acknowledge and applaud those designers whose work appears in *NatureCrafts*.

We are sure that there are craftsmen and observers of nature other than the ones we name here who have come to similar designs and conclusions. But it is the following fine, sensitive individuals to whom we are particularly grateful—both for the opportunity to know them and for sharing their talents and love of nature with us.

SpringCrafts

SummerCrafts

AutumnCrafts

WinterCrafts

continued . . .

WinterCrafts continued

Suppliers

One of the beauties of our country is the wealth of natural resources peculiar to each locale. Gulf Coast residents are inundated with many beautiful seashells, but they may long for pine cones found only in the West. And while your hometown may not have a supplier for your felting or paper-making projects, a larger city may have several companies eager to help you.

The following list of suppliers is offered to make what may be hard-to-find materials available to every craftsman. To avoid unnecessary confusion regarding prices, availability of materials, or shipping charges, first contact the supplier with whom you wish to do business and request complete ordering information.

SpringCrafts

8-15 FELT: NATURE'S TEXTILE—raw wool, processed wool, and carded fleece
Dharma Trading Company
1918 University Avenue
Berkeley, California 94704
(Raw and processed wool)

Dream Weaver
2980 Grandview Avenue, N.E.
Atlanta, Georgia 30305
(Raw and processed wool)

Halcyon: The Weaver's Friend
1121 California Street
Denver, Colorado 80204
(Processed wool and carded fleece)

Harrisville Designs
P.O. Box 51
Harrisville, New Hampshire 03450
(Processed wool and carded fleece)

Shepherd's Harvest
1925 Central Street
Evanston, Illinois 60201
(Raw and processed wool)

SummerCrafts

24-37 SEASHELLS: JEWELS FROM THE SEA—seashells
Benjane Arts
320 Hempstead Avenue
West Hempstead, New York 11552
(40-page color catalog: $3.00)

She Sells Sea Shells
1983 Periwinkle Way
Sanibel Island, Florida 33957

27-29 SEASHELL NECKLACES—jewelry findings
Eastern Findings Corporation
19 West 34th Street
New York, New York 10001
(Minimum order: $15.00 in quantities of 1 gross)

Florida Supply House, Inc.
P.O. Box 847
Bradenton, Florida 33506
(Catalog: $1.00. Minimum order: $10.00)

AutumnCrafts

WinterCrafts

Index

continued . . .